At Least Next Week I'm on Vacation

By

Danny Roberts

Gathered Thoughts Books
Published by Indigo Sea Press
Winston-Salem

Gathered Thoughts Books
Indigo Sea Press
302 Ricks Drive
Winston-Salem, NC 27103

First Gathered Thoughts Books edition published
December, 2015
Gathered Thoughts Books, Moon Sailor and all production design are trademarks of Indigo Sea Press, used under license.

For information regarding bulk purchases of this book, digital purchase and special discounts, please contact the publisher at indigoseapress.com

Cover design by Stacy Castanedo

Manufactured in the United States of America
ISBN 978-1-63066-236-3

To Brenda Kay

Acknowledgments

I'd like to thank Christy Vance and Robin Chalkley for their invaluable input and patience.

Table of Contents

Remember, Stay Calm

His stride was short, almost mincing for a man his size. But there was no doubting his destination or purpose as each step brought him closer to me. His shoulders were wide and his chest strained the fabric of his plain white t-shirt. The muscled arms that looked like they could make my knees buckle if he merely laid one around my shoulders, flexed as he pounded one giant fist into open palm.

I thought I had reached the stage in my life where inner peace, wisdom, and diplomacy had rendered me incapable of honestly and totally pissing someone off. I was wrong. The behemoth hurrying toward my car with the intention introducing my eyeballs to my anus reminded me I still had that skill. It was not a happy revelation.

Of all the bad things that could happen while driving, like getting lost, running out of gas, and getting eaten by coyotes, my greatest fear is plunging my truck off the side of a tall bridge into a body of cold, deep water. My ability to swim will never measure up to my ability to drown. This is yet unproven, but I don't need proof. I sense it and believe, like faith in a higher power.

When crossing a high bridge with water waiting to greet me below I settle my nerves with how quick-thinking and emotionless I'd be if the worst happened. My Mitsubishi flying through the air in a graceful arc, I would roll down the window before we hit the water, calmly unbuckle my seatbelt, slither out the open window, and then flounder around long enough for a passing lifeguard, on his way home from work, to drag me sputtering to shore. It would be a nice story at eleven. He would be a hero, photographed smiling and proud. I would be standing beside him, wrapped in a blanket and looking like an over-sized otter but not as cute. This is fine by me because I would be alive and happy, although I'd miss my truck. In reality, of course, between the screaming and praying, I'd never

1

get that window rolled down or seatbelt unbuckled. In real life everything happens so damn fast, like the guy reaching for my door handle at that very moment.

Up close, I could see my new friend's nose had been flattened somewhere in his rowdy past. It separated two small eyes that somehow stayed cold in that large hot head. His hair was cut short, and spiked to sharp points that could pop a balloon. The prototypical big and ugly. These are the types of people I try to avoid severe conversations with. I would have locked my door and stuck my tongue out at him except my door lock has been broken since Halloween. Twenty dollars and your little head can lead you places the rest of you should never follow. That trick was no treat. I looked for an escape.

Big Ugly's car was directly in front of me. I checked the rearview mirror and a U-Haul truck was crowding me from behind; no room there. The driver of the U-Haul was simultaneously eating a Whopper and picking his nose, with the same hand. I admire dexterity but there was no time to watch this now. To my right, in a Volkswagen, sat a teenage girl who appeared to be praying for me, but she was actually texting, probably to a friend, something like, "*OMG Step u shd c d drama rite bside me!*" To my left was the barrier wall. I was trapped but I had an idea.

The best defense is a good offense. I flung open the door, which caught the big ape off guard. He rightly had me pegged for a coward, so this was unexpected. Because the wall was so close, the door would only open halfway. Perfect! I jammed both feet against the inside door panel and it hit the wall with a bang. That was going to leave a mark I maybe could buff out later. I was more concerned that some things would be done to me that couldn't be so easily repaired.

Despite his strength, Big Ugly didn't have enough leverage to push the door back. With a yell, he tore around the front of the truck to the other side. The lock on that door, thankfully, still worked. "Aha, you evil miscreant," my voice sounded shaky and strange. "Locked!" He ran around the back of my truck coming for me at a different angle. I slammed my door shut and fumbled with the glove compartment latch, looking for a weapon.

Safe driving habits are so hard to acquire and so easy to ignore. We speed, cut other drivers off, do rolling stops at stop signs, get distracted by girls in short shorts. It's pathetic, really. To the good driving habits of keeping your eyes on the road and both hands on the wheel, I'd like to add do not honk your horn unnecessarily long and loud, and don't use vulgar hand signals. Especially if the receiver of these gestures is a tall man with a short temper who takes the same exit you do and pulls in front of you at a red light. It could save a life.

I thrashed through the items in my glove box: owner's manual, registration, receipts, a postcard from Charles Manson...what!? No that's Charles *Mason*, my Nationwide Insurance agent. Wow, Tahiti really is beautiful. My hand closed around a piece of metal, a bottle opener from Cedar Island. What wonderful memories it brings back; me and my baby cruising down Highway 12 popping tops off Coronas, listening to Big Head Todd and the Monsters, during a more carefree time. There was a fold-out corkscrew on the other end of the opener. It was this or nothing.

He jerked my door open and it slammed into the divider wall a second time. That mark wasn't going to buff out as easily. Thank God for that wall though, it most likely saved my life because I dropped the bottle opener.

Big Ugly grabbed me by my shirt and tried to drag me through the door, but my seatbelt was still fastened. Another safe-driving tip: wear your seatbelt at all times. He tried to punch me with his free hand but because of his size and the small opening in the door, he couldn't get a clean shot. Plus, I was all pumped up on adrenaline and fear so I was as quick as a mongoose, bobbing and weaving, dodging most of his blows. But since he was determined and at least smart enough to operate a motor vehicle, albeit badly, I figured in a manner of seconds he might actually think of a new technique.

"I'll teach you to flip me off, you cocksucker!" He yelled. I wanted to tell him a couple of things. First, there are no cocksuckers in our lineage, if you discount the cousin in Tennessee, and second, I had learned today's lesson and needed no more tutoring. But I was apparently in the company of someone who believes in higher education, because he kept yanking on me with one hand and trying to flail on me with the other. The red light finally turned green.

The U-Haul driver, finished with his boogers and his burger, started honking his horn. I didn't have time to see if he was using the same hand or not. I also don't know what he thought was happening in front of him, but keeping the traffic moving in an orderly fashion was way low on both Big Ugly's and my own priority list. He unhanded me, yelled, "Screw you asshole!" to the U-Haul driver and gave him the finger.

I used this brief timeout to pick up the bottle opener, when he reached for me again, I stabbed him in the palm with the corkscrew and, for good measure, gave it a good twist. He cried out, staggered backwards against the wall, and grabbed his chest with his bloody hand, leaving a big red stain on his shirt. He was a changed man. Moments before he looked like an angry beet, now he was all pale, his face pasty. "This is interesting," I thought.

"He's been shot!" I heard a woman scream.

"Puh-leeze," I said. "He's having a heart attack." He was obviously a Type A personality. Why do some people try to sensationalize everything?

"It's not a gunshot wound it's a corkscrew wound. I want that back by the way, it has sentimental value."

Big Ugly looked at me blankly, uncomprehending, but I saw fear in his eyes because he knew now I meant business. "The worm has turned, mon frère, au revoir, and let up on the French fries." I reached down to where he had fallen against the wall, uncorked him, wiped the blood off on my jeans, and to the blasting horns of even more angry motorists, pulled around and drove off.

Somewhere in the distance I heard the wail of a siren and wondered if it was for him or for me.

It's in the Stars, Really!

I don't know how it was on your street last night, but at my house the sky was sharp and clear, the stars unusually bright. As God as my witness, I swear it was not chemically-induced. My wife looked up into that beautiful sky and, as she sometimes does, started showing off by naming the constellations. Yep, she's one of those people.

Apparently constellations have been around for thousands of years and no one really knows why. But we'll blame it on the ancient Greeks, mainly because they're not around to defend themselves. Perhaps one cloudless evening Socrates nudged his friend in the ribs and pointed skyward. "Enough with all the philosophizing, Plato, look at the sky."

Plato sagely stroked his beard and looked up. "Yes?"

"The stars, they have patterns. Doesn't that look like a fish?" Socrates traced with his finger. "Look over there; doesn't that appear to be a virgin?"

"How would you know what a virgin looks like?" Plato, who enjoys a good joke as much as the next great thinker, was getting into the spirit of the evening. He sees nothing unusual about tonight's sky, especially virgins and fish.

"We must name them, Plato."

"Of course."

"…and share our discovery with the world."

"Obviously."

Thus began a joke that has lasted for centuries. Older even than strippers telling you they're working their way through college.

Since only a select few of very special people claim to see these silver etchings against the ultimate blue canvas, they must maintain their little secret society, perpetuating the joke. They gather at Taco Bell and over a Smothered Burrito or three they laugh and laugh. "Last week," says one, "I convinced some mouth-breather that there was a winged horse in the sky where

I was pointing. He actually said he saw it. God, that was hilarious. What an idiot."

But, you see, they can't trick me anymore because I'm on to them. I just nod politely and say "sure do" when they ask if I see Mesopotamia, Sacagawea, and Kournikova (now there's a heavenly body), or Taurus. I'm not lying either, because I did see a Taurus yesterday with a dent in the left front fender, and a bumper sticker that read, "Don't fear the reefer". The astute among them know I'm pulling their leg and I admit I could maybe make out an ornate walking stick amongst the stars if I stared really hard. They look sad then, shake their heads at the ungifted, "There are none so blind..." their eyes seem to say.

They break from their meetings and venture among us. There could be twenty people sharing adult beverages on the outdoor patio, innocently talking sports, politics, or slinging mud about mutual acquaintances that are conveniently absent, when one of them will invariably say, "Look there's Old Ryan." A few guests will turn suddenly, looking guilty because they've been talking about "Old Ryan's" propensity to get falling down drunk lately, then they realize the speaker is looking skyward. She's talking about "Orion".

I don't trouble myself trying to connect those shiny little dots. Instead I check out the people who think they can scare up an image. With necks craned they look so sincere, trying so hard to see something that's not there, much like the usefulness of a Kardashian. Eventually one says, and another, and then another, "There it is and it's lovely tonight." The soul of a rube is the fear of looking stupid.

Standing under a midnight-blue sky certainly beats watching television so once again I'm by my wife's side and once again she's up to her tomfoolery. "Look," she says, so earnest it's almost heartbreaking, "Don't you see it? There's the hunter, his sword, see his arms and legs? There's his head. When did he get his ear pierced?" She doesn't see anything either or maybe she thinks she does, which is another, more worrisome issue. But she won't let go of that joke. But neither would I if I could get away with it.

And My Socks Don't Match Either

If you're a man, and you know if you are, you understand how tricky fashion can be. There's that line between trying to look acceptable and not caring at all. Thankfully, the line isn't thin—we can wander a bit before our women either crack down or give up on us. I'm thinking the boundaries are somewhere between wearing sweat pants to church and carrying a man purse.

The New York Times says men are accessorizing more now that the economy is getting better. They didn't say better for who but this was *The New York Times* and they only say what Obama wants them to say; besides the article was about fashion. Apparently men have started wearing bracelets, called "wrist wear" and sporting purses, called "hold-alls" to give the impression they are more "put together" and "polished." This is supposed to impress their employer or even help them land a job. It never occurred to me, back when I was unemployed, that a few dangly bracelets, a purse, a scarf tied around my neck just so, and a fedora would land me my dream job at Jiffy Lube.

"Hey Dan, you got that three-quarter inch socket wrench?"

"Yeah Slim, it's right there, under my purse." Wow, the things you can learn from *The New York Times*.

I used to subscribe to *Men's Health* magazine with the intention of following its profound advice to a leaner, healthier me. Without consciously realizing it, I started reading this magazine less and less. I thought it was because of my natural ability to be stupendously lazy until a friend saw a copy lying on my coffee table and asked me why I was reading a gay magazine. "Now wait a damn minute here buckaroo," I said in my deepest voice. "What makes you think that's a gay magazine?"

He pointed out that most of the articles were about style and grooming, not about building muscle. Damn the luck. He had a point. I wanted to know how to have six-pack abs, not which color socks to wear to a late-afternoon cocktail party after Labor Day. There was even an article about shaving. What am I, fifteen? One of the few things I can do correctly is *shave*. If you miss a whisker mister is it a fashion faux pas? I tossed that male version of *Elle* into the trash. A tree died for that? I wept. Nah, just kidding.

Not all men are accessorizing of course, just the ones with style and pizazz. You know who you are. I don't personally fraternize with any of these men, we don't have the same interests or life goals. Then again, I'm not around my friends twenty-four seven so they could be dressed to the nines when I'm not around. I do know if their socks match they feel like they're looking pretty doggone sporty.

I did a personal inventory and surprised myself. I wear a ring, wedding in nature, a necklace that I think is cool, and a watch. Apparently these are accessories all and here I thought I was just wearing a watch, a necklace, and a ring. It must be semantics. No earrings though. This is my limit. I'm nowhere near cool enough for that.

For all of her fashion sense, sometimes I still have to explain to my wife that when I throw on a shirt and pair pants that unexpectedly match, this is not an "outfit" it's a shirt and a pair of pants. Most men don't wear outfits, not without a matching purse, they don't. Sometimes a man shows up in a certain place, performing a task, wearing clothes specific to that task or activity that match. If it's his job, it's a uniform. If it's a leisurely pursuit, well doggone it, I guess it is an outfit.

Yesterday I was sitting in my car at a stoplight trying to decide which nostril to favor first with my finger when a couple of rodeo clowns came trotting by. This is not a normal everyday occurrence. I was intrigued and eagerly anticipated the bull following close behind with a snort and clatter of hooves. The bull didn't show, the light turned green, and as I pulled away I saw that they weren't rodeo clowns at all; they were joggers. My bad, but they were certainly dressed like rodeo clowns, and except for the face paint, they could easily have been scampering for a fence or hiding in a barrel.

The joggers were just a couple of guys wearing "shorts" that fell just below the knee, over red tights no less, lime green and lemon jackets, red sweatbands, and gloves in some shade of purple. I take it they wanted to be seen by motorists and avoid being flattened before they reached their optimum heart rate, but the fact they were jogging on the sidewalk lessened the chances of this happening considerably. "There it is," I thought. "There's the reason I'm not an elite athlete or at least able to climb a flight of stairs without prayer." I don't want to look any goofier than I already do.

I realize at a certain age a man should give up the AC/DC t-shirt, but I'm still slightly confounded that people appear in public dressed in something I'd be embarrassed to wear in my home, with the lights turned off.

I suppose it's that way with any sport or hobby that requires an "outfit." Since I swore off golf years ago, reasoning that I have enough aggravation without paying for it, I didn't know if the participants still wore those ugly pants or not. I accidently saw John Daly on TV the other day and judging by what he had on, the answer is yes, they most certainly do. Of course he is a professional and he gets paid to wear those pants. If someone chooses to wear them for free, they're just asking to get beaned by a Titleist.

Then there are the cyclists. It takes more courage than I can possibly muster to ride around on a bicycle with spandex on your butt and what looks like a large turtle on your head. That's why I slow down and give them a wide berth when I get ready to pass them on the road. If I accidently ran one over I'd have to stop, call 911, wait for the ambulance, and possibly try to administer aid and comfort. It's the right thing to do, but all this time I'd have to look at them. Those tight-fitting shirts bursting at the seams, those shorts with the unsightly bulges; like I told the 911 operator, "It's too horrible to describe." Besides, my wife is a cyclist and I don't want to run her over for more

9

reasons than this page will hold.

I do feel I am qualified to give one bit of fashion advice. "If you feel compelled to ridicule the clothes of a person who can kill you—think about it first." Let's say a storm has inconveniently dropped a large oak tree into your kitchen and the whole family agreed that you should go get breakfast. You find yourself standing in a McDonald's at six AM on a Saturday morning thinking about homeowner's insurance. You may encounter a hunter there. An outdoorsman dressed head to toe in camouflage except for an orange vest. You don't tell such a person that you "like his outfit." He may only have a compound bow in his pickup but you can bet your ass he knows how to use it. Take your frappe, avert your eyes, and walk silently to the car. I do.

Jogging and riding a bicycle is obviously good for you. And hunting helps thin out the herd, both the animals and men who are not wearing bright orange vests. Golf, even if it is just riding around in an electric cart drinking beer, is still more exercise than I get from just running my mouth daily. This activity doesn't require me to dress funny, though I do anyway.

Fashion, to me, is like soccer. It's foreign, it's boring, and I already know all I want to know about it; which is pretty much next to nothing. My fashion rules are very simple: Never overdress and don't wear pajama bottoms to go shopping. If I ever roll out of bed one morning, grab my keys, wallet, and cell phone but forget my pants, I have a bigger problem than worrying about being dapper. If I stray too far from my own personal boundaries, my wife, the fashion cop, cracks down on me.

"You're not wearing that are you?" she asks.

"Well, I was planning to."

"No, not with me you're not."

I thought stripes and plaids were okay to wear together these days. At least they weren't pajama bottoms.

As tricky as fashion can be, there are still some calls that are easy to make. When it comes to tights and spandex for instance, good-looking women not only get a bye, it's encouraged. Especially by men sitting at stoplights, pondering their next big decision. And that, ladies, that ain't no bull.

You've Got Mail Damn It!

My computer most certainly is a female. I know what you're thinking, "It's a machine, dummy." But trust me, only a woman could cause me this much damn grief.

Every day it's drama. Every day it's an adventure. I don't want adventure. I don't want drama from my computer. I want to be able to do something besides play solitaire four to six hours a day. The thing I desire most in my life is another way to waste time.

I have friends who tell me their computers have opened up a new and wonderful world to them, that computers are useful tools. They write bad stories, watch movies, and play games. They chat with their other little friends on line. It's all so sweet. I don't believe the lying shits for a second. If it was so easy anybody could do it.

Yesterday I tried to download a very interesting and informative video about someone stepping into the street while texting and getting flattened by a city bus. I bet he didn't even know what hit him. But I can only speculate on how very amusing this video was because my computer just sat there and looked at me. "Why are you touching me there?" she seemed to be saying. Just when I think I've got her figured out and we're going to get along, she changes, becomes difficult without a hint of what is wrong. I'm just supposed to know. Now you tell me that ain't a woman.

I feel like I'm looking at one of those pictures that has another image hidden it. To see that image you have to cross your eyes and make everything blurry. There are a bunch of people standing around and after a few minutes they all say, "I see it. It's Mother Teresa picking her nose." Now I don't see no shit like that but I don't want to be the only one that doesn't so I say, "Yeah, yeah there it is and she's got that thing buried up to the second knuckle too. Goodness."

Truth is, if got stranded on a deserted island with nothing to look at but that picture I'd still be scratching my head. I could slip into delirium and Mother Teresa appear, with one hand gently on my shoulder saying, "Look my child and you shall see." I'd be saying, "Nope, I don't get it." There are some things that I wasn't meant to understand.

Like these e-mails that keep popping up in my in box. I'm getting e-mails from Venus. No, not the planet, not yet anyway. Apparently Venus is some company that makes swimwear for women. Now why are they sending me e-mails about enhancer tops and scoop bottoms? Does that sound like something I need to wiggle my hairy ass into?

Then there's some place called The Alzheimer's Store. I've tried to block the sender and have their e-mail sent directly to the junk mail file, but they're still there. I even e-mailed them back, pleading with them to please stop sending me notices because I don't think I have Alzheimer's anymore. I may in the future need some products from their store but by then I won't be aware of it so they're just wasting everybody's time.

I asked my friend Steve, who is a computer guru but I call him Steve, "Why can't I put an end to all this unwanted electronic mail? Is it something I'm doing wrong?"

"Well," he said. "It could be you're not transferring the logitherms from your data setback through your aerial feeder with a pre-scripted scepter foil. This is trebling the outtake and over-extending the ringworm through its own gravitational link. I hope I didn't over-simplify that."

"No, no, not at all." I assured him. I had no idea what in the hell Steve just said but I wasn't about to admit it. He already thinks I put the dumb in dumbass. Realizing that a slow-witted eight-year-old would have understood that nonsense perfectly I slinked back to my computer and did what I always do when she gives me fits. I pounded on the keyboard with both fists and yelled obscenities at the monitor. This just seemed to cause more problems. I guess those bumper stickers were right, violence really isn't the answer.

As I sit there, sweaty and despondent, the cheery bell chimes through my computer's speakers, signaling that Mr.

Electronic Mailman has delivered some more good news. When I open up the mailbox, "Well, well, what is this?" The Alzheimer's Store has sent me another chatty little note. They were hoping that I had forgotten I don't have Alzheimer's and would order the no-start car battery or the four-piece jigsaw puzzle. I pounded on the keyboard some more and wondered what I did for aggravation before computers came along.

Let me see...Oh yeah, I remember trying to squeeze my fingers thorough that tiny little flap door of the VCR attempting to scrape the broken VHS tape off the heads with a butter knife. I was making a futile effort to piece it back together so the video rental store wouldn't make me buy the damn thing. It was that lousy Gary Busey movie. You know the one I'm talking about. The movie with the kid in the souped-up wheelchair with the werewolves chasing him all around. Yeah, it was as stupid as it sounds.

Then there was the time I taped a stack of nickels to the arm of my turntable to keep it from skipping across my favorite Gran Funk Railroad album, ruining the drum solo. Those were the days I tell you.

Now people are asking me if I will friend them on something called Facefrigginbook so I can be privy to such awe-inspiring information as "I just shaved my crotch and will be doing naked handstands in front of my window until nine o'clock. I still live at 902 Hysteria Lane BTW, LOL, and FU2. Hit like if you agree." Have you ever heard such shit in your life? Or maybe Farmville is your thing there, coyote breath. "Maurice just found a bushel basket full of sno-cones and shoved a turnip up his ass." I never dreamed I would ever actually miss Gary Busey.

But this e-mail problem is what makes my trigger-finger itch. There's some persistent chick that's dying to sell me Avon. Now please, there's not enough makeup on this planet to make me pretty. Is this woman possibly insane? You know the internet is full of nutjobs preying on innocent fifty-eight-year-old men.

I thought she had my e-mail mixed up with my wife's.

Maybe she was a friend or possibly a client. "Honey, do you know someone named Suzy Lafloozie?" I asked.

"Sounds like one of your old girlfriends to me." She replied.

Now I know my wife knows this is not true and she is just being a smartass but how can I prove it when apparently I'm one of The Alzheimer Store's best customers?

Malevolently Yours

In the old days, in much simpler times when people weren't as sophisticated, it was a pain in the ass to hate someone. Expensive and time-consuming, people really had to go out of their way to fully express their loathing for one another.

For instance, when our country first started really getting cranked up, we had to kill a bunch of British to win our freedom, earning the right to hate whatever group of people we wanted without being told by a monarch. This is why some countries hate us today. Jealousy.

After the British we were forced to kill the French, the Indians, and then the British all over again. It was a mess. By this time many Americans were tired of war, prompting a truce to be called and they were able to enjoy up to six full months of peace. Since there was no NFL or MMA to watch on TV, civilized people met at social gatherings called soirees. They were called soirees because someone made up the word before considering what it was going to be used for. "What the hell," they thought, "Everyone loves a party. If we start calling them soirees everyone will love my new word too." And they did. Sorta. The results were mixed.

Now that people had, at least temporarily, stopped blowing each other to bits with cannons and muskets, they had time to throw back a toddy or two, dance minuets, and play a little grab ass. They partied until their wigs got all cockeyed and then they went home. They were, after all, civilized. But since some people back then couldn't hold their liquor any better than some people today, occasionally tempers were lost and feelings were hurt, very much like the last time my family got together for Christmas.

Abigail Henry, of colonial Williamsburg, was one of those people who should have never taken a drink. Normally quiet and reserved, she became quite mouthy and a little bit of a slut when she had thrown back a few. She and her husband, Joseph, were attending a function at the home of Mr. William Moore but left the party in a huff and rode back to the plantation in silence. Joseph, a prideful man, stewed for days about the goings on at that damn soiree, and since he knew his letters, decided to use some of them. Finally able to raise the right amount of indignation, he sat down with ink and quill and composed an angry message:

Mr. William Moore,

I am frightfully disappointed in your behavior at the last social event my wife and I attended at your home. I find your conduct reprehensible and unbecoming of a gentleman. It was brought to my attention that you clumsily groped, not once, but several times, my wife's rosy bottom. I demand an apology forthwith and will indeed get satisfaction before the sun rises on a new year.

Yep, them were fightin' words. Mr. Henry stormed down to the local post office to mail his letter. He was pretty tuckered out by the time he got there because he had been so mad when he left that he forgot his horse. The "local" post office was four miles away. A man can go through a lot of changes during a four mile walk. At mile two he wasn't even sure if he was mad anymore and by mile three he had forgotten why he was mad to begin with. But the Henrys were from hardy stock and, by God, that letter was getting mailed.

Three months later, Mr. William Moore was elated to receive a letter from his good friend Joseph Henry but was taken aback by the content. "Goodness," he said aloud. "What kind of tomfoolery is this? If Joe Henry thinks I had a hand in feeling his wife's plump rear end, he's made a dire mistake. I'll show him he's in no position to demand anything."

Mr. Moore mulled this over for a while and then sat down and wrote his own little message. Six months later, Mr. Henry was overjoyed to find a letter from his good friend William waiting at the post office. "It will be so good to hear from him," he told the owner of the general store. "I hope he's invited us to another of his splendid soirees. Duel! He's challenged me to a duel?"

17

Nonplussed but no coward, Joseph Henry agreed to the duel one year to the day after the alleged butt-grabbing incident. Since roads were terrible and there was no GPS to rely on, both parties got hopelessly lost on the way to the neutral site they had agreed on. Mr. Henry was captured by a group of angry Native Americans and was given an extremely close haircut. Mr. Moore, meanwhile, stumbled bleary-eyed and starving into a frontier town, where he was mistaken for a wanted killer and was hung by the neck until dead. It was a mess.

Thankfully the telephone came along helping you avoid blunders such as these, but more importantly, making it much easier to convey how pissed off you are. You picked up your rotary dial, waited for the party line to clear, and then you and your neighbor screamed obscenities at each other. After the insults petered out, you got to slam down the phone with immense satisfaction. "I guess I told her." You said, while on the other end your neighbor said, "I guess I told her." This was indeed progress, but problems loomed ahead in the form of more progress.

On the heels of the telephone came answering machines and caller ID. People were able to screen their calls, taking away the instant gratification of calling someone an asshole while their slight was still fresh on your nerves. You could leave a hideously vulgar message without being hung up on but it just wasn't the same as a good old shouting match. With caller ID someone could pick up the phone, see who was calling and just ignore you. There's nothing worse than being ignored when you're mad. My wife taught me this.

Anyway, answering machines caused Americans who were merely irate to become homicidal, shooting their blood pressure through the stratosphere. Heart attacks became an epidemic and insurance premiums staggered the economy. Thank God the internet came along. Al Gore should be the fifth face on Mount Rushmore.

How nice is it now to be able to insult, berate, and degrade someone with the mere click of a button? How pleasant to ridicule their vacation pictures on Facebook or destroy their self-esteem with 140 characters or less on Twitter. You don't even have to have a grasp of the English language to get your jabs in. It's beautiful in its simplicity.

There's no risk of someone calling you illiterate because most of the people you're trading barbs with don't know you're illiterate. With Twitter, Facebook, Skype, texting, and e-mail, there are a myriad of ways to trash talk without getting punched in the nose, tied to a whipping post or put in stocks. It's amazing all the ways you can converse without being able to carry on a conversation, and really, isn't that what communication is all about?

Instant gratification has made the world a better place. Gone are the days of waiting hours, weeks, or even months to let someone know exactly how you feel. Boy, I'd be pretty pissed off if I had to get in my car, drive all the way down to the post office, and buy a stamp to tell somebody I hated their guts. Who has time for that?

So That's Where Navels Come From

It's not that I have anything against pregnant women, not really. They do tend to take up a lot of room but when you consider that only 3.23% of women of childbearing age are pregnant at one time and over 35% of Americans are obese all the time, that's not a valid reason not to like them. Besides they are much like the playful creatures we pay to see at Sea World, but out among us, at no cost. Amusing and delightful, they do unexpected tricks, like stooping to tie their shoes.

It's not that I'm worried about being trapped alone with one when she suddenly goes into labor, either. I'd never allow this to happen. There's not a category of coward that I don't fall under. Supposedly "feel good" stories pop up to horrify me from time to time; a policeman, a cab driver, some random stranger bravely helping deliver a new life into this world. Good for them. I have my own plan of action if a woman who looks like she's going to explode with fetus grabs her belly and moans, "I think it's time!" I'll run screaming into the night, "She's having a baby! She's having a baby! For the love of God, somebody help me find the nearest bar?!" So you won't see a picture of me in The Daily Trite posing with the exhausted mother and shell shocked papa.

They say pregnant women have that certain glow. This could be, but personally, it sounds a mite suspicious for someone in abject misery being happy enough to glow. The glow is actually a sheen, especially in the dog days of August; a sheen that covers all of the exposed areas on their bodies. It's merely a good healthy sweat worked up as they trundle along with their feet splayed outward, their shoulders pitched back, and their arms canted to the sides like the twin hulls of a catamaran. I'm not jealous of that glow, you know.

Sometimes parents read Shakespeare and Hemingway to

their little fetuses. When junior learns to talk he'll say things like, "There are no friends as loyal as a book" and "It is not in the stars to hold our destiny but in ourselves." This will make him extremely popular in gym class. The expectant couple listens to classical music and NPR, all in an attempt to be a good influence on the child before birth. They dream of little Ryker or Brylee growing up to drive a Volvo, listen to Vivaldi, and play croquet on manicured lawns; spending Sunday afternoons attending first showings of up and coming artists.

These things weigh heavily on my mind when my job takes me to Women's Hospital several times a week. There, I encounter small herds of these beings much different than myself. Some are there only with their husbands or their baby's daddy. Others treat it as the social event of the season. Their mamas and daddies are there, their sisters and brothers, and brothers and sister-in-laws, grandma, grandpa, Aunt Merle and Uncle Norman, the gardener, and Chavez the lawyer. The only thing missing is the picnic basket. All waiting for the water to break. Sorta strange if you ask me, but then again, they didn't invite me or my opinion.

But while merely doing my job, sometimes I'm approached by one of these women, looking as if she recently swallowed Jupiter, who mistakenly thinks I work at the hospital. They're looking for a bathroom or the snack machine. I look at her belly and think of that little person, an unseen specter that's been subjected to the finer things of life, and I just lower my head and say quietly, "I don't know."

If I start speaking to these women in my normal vernacular, their child will not follow the course that was planned for it. There will be no country clubs or Wall Street. Ryker will insist on being called "Bubba" as he squeals out of the driveway, spitting tobacco juice out the window of his pick-up truck, with Bochephus blaring on the stereo, on his way to get a new tattoo. The poor parents will wring their hands and lament, "Where did we go wrong?" Of course eventually they will turn on one another, placing blame and there will be yet another one-parent household. All because I said, "Now wait a minute hot mama. What makes you think I know where the snack machine is? Do I look like I have nothing better to do than stand around all day directing chunky monkeys to their next feeding? Besides it looks like you've had enough Cheetos."

It's not that I have anything against pregnant women, not really. I just can't stand the thought of someone in camouflage britches walking up to me and saying, "I want to thank you, man, for helping me turn out the way I did. You want a Slim Jim?"

It's Italian

Sometimes I forget I'm married and try to assert my manhood. I'll get a little cocky, shoot off my mouth, maybe even push my luck and stay out past nine o'clock with my friends. My wife knows how to get even though; she fixes me a fine home-cooked Italian meal.

"Guess what we're having for dinner tonight, honey?" She calls from the kitchen to the unusual accompaniment of rattling pots and pans.

I don't have to guess, I know. I can hear the glee in her voice. We're having some kind of meat, destroyed by marinara sauce, some configuration of noodles, and parmesan cheese. Linguine, fettuccini, baked ziti, or rigatoni-it's all the same to me.

But she usually whips up a batch of lasagna. It's my favorite. I like food that has enough cheese in it to constipate a Clydesdale. Lasagna has a presence that fills the room. It knows that I don't like it and it doesn't like me. It almost speaks. "Come on. Say something with your wife sitting right over there. I dare you. Now take a big bite, big man." So I nibble on a corner, and I smile across the table.

"Yummy," My wife says. "Isn't this lasagna delicious?"

She's right of course. I mean, gosh, how could chunks of cardboard slathered in tomato paste not be? How many times have garlic bread and salad saved me from starvation? But at least she doesn't make me go to Olive Garden, where appetites go to die.

I hear people say, "Ooooh, I just love Olive Garden." They've just never met a lie they didn't like. I suspect they also have pictures of Bigfoot, or channel the spirit of Elvis at Christmas. Come to think of it I've never heard a couple say they love Olive Garden, it's usually just the female. This is where the wife takes the husband to punish him for forgotten birthdays and anniversaries. I wonder how many couples have broken up with their forks hovering over a dish of eggplant parmigiana?

I feel like I'm getting gypped when I eat Italian. I'm not talking about portion sizes. I'm talking about imagination. The only difference in Italian dishes is the shape of the noodles. It's like a big game of "pretend". "So you don't like the corkscrew-shaped noodles in tomato sauce? Let me bring you some shell-shaped noodles covered in tomato sauce. Better?"

"Yes, much. Thank you."

I'll be sitting in a restaurante Italiano, obnoxious accordion music piped in especially for my enjoyment, trying to remember the name of a dish that didn't make me puke last time I visited. The waiter approaches, carrying a cheese grater, and asks me what I'll have. "Well, I kinda like that thing with the noodles that are shaped like little wagon wheels. They have spokes and everything."

"I see, sir. Would you possibly be interested in actually eating this dish or would you prefer to merely play with your food?"

"Now that you mention it..." My wife kicks me underneath the table. "Uh, what would something like that be called?"

"Sir, if I may recommend, 'something like that' would be called "Casseruola di Rotelle e con Polpettine Salsiccia."

"Yep, that's it all right." I say.

I grew up on beans and taters, fried chicken, biscuits, and sweet tea. My wife, who is not from around here but a fine individual all the same, will sometimes prepare this meal for me and call it "comfort food". I still call it "supper". I rave and smack my lips over this special meal because I know, lurking in the cabinet, there be noodles.

I'm not strictly Pro-American when it comes feeding my face. I like Chinese, Japanese, and Thai food. Although, to be honest, I can't tell them apart and I'm just trying to pad my case with geographical names from the Far East. But I do eat Greek and Mexican food on a regular basis. As a matter of fact they help keep me regular. It could be the lack of cheese. So I think I'm fairly open-minded about what I eat.

In the foreign city my wife hails from, Cleveland, they eat something called kielbasa. It's interesting, especially when you throw in that sauerkraut they're so crazy about up that way. The also like to grill brats, which turns out to be a fancy hot dog. When I was younger a brat was someone who got their ass busted in church. Now the only buns getting warmed are the ones beside the "brats", on the grill.

My mother was a fine Southern cook. She took simple recipes and turned them into a feast. That's why all of her children eventually took on the shape of plump watermelons. She never whipped up any rigatoni or manicotti though. If you wanted Italian you opened up a can of Chef Boyardee beefaroni or ravioli. My goodness how I learned to hate the mustached smiling face on that can. Still though, I'm surprised he doesn't have his own reality cooking show.

He could come out with a variety of can openers and his vast array of fine canned pasta products and, along with some light bread, plop some on a paper plate for one of his celebrity guests. Someone like Paris Hilton or maybe the Duchess of Cambridge.

"Eww," They'd whine, turning up their cultured noses. "I don't like this. I can't eat this."

But Chef Boyardee knows his audience. He turns to his snotty guests and says what all over-worked, harried mothers have wanted to say through the years, "You'll eat it when you get hungry enough." Or the crowd favorite, "You can eat it or you can wear it." Paris and Kate's mouths fly open in shock and the live audience stands and cheers. "Wear it, wear it, wear it!" They chant. As the show goes to a commercial, Kate runs off the stage with a big orange splotch of cheap tomato sauce on the front of her pearl Alexander McQueen frock. Oh, what entertainment that would be. Finally a reality show I could relate to.

I don't have a tattoo but if I did it would say, "American by birth and Southern by the grace of God." That's a lot of letters and each one carrying a heap of pain I imagine. But it would be the gastronomic equivalent of a medical alert bracelet. Say I've been lost in the wilderness for days. Finally I'm found by Denise and my friend, Luigi. I'm half-starved, nearly passed out from hunger.

Denise runs to me and throws herself on my prone body, normally this is a good thing but now is not the time. I try to talk.

"What's he saying Luigi?" She implores, one hand reaching skyward. It's a very dramatic scene.

"He says he's hungry, very hungry."

"Here, we have food. Give him some of this spinach parmesan crostini."

"No Denise," Luigi says, gently pulling her away. "See his tattoo? Never mind the crostini. I think he'd rather die."

My Little Dictators

I was taking a leak in the back yard the other day when my neighbor's wife came outside to water her daffodils. Though I waved vigorously with my free hand, she didn't respond at all. She had to have seen me-she was staring right at me. This is not how neighbors act in civilized society, she could have at least attempted to be friendly. She's always been a stuck-up sort though for no discernible reason I can see. Through extensive research and some carefully worded inquiries I found out she used to be a stripper, and God knows what else, out in Vegas. So she can drop the Little Miss My Poop Don't Smell act anytime. I told my wife about it, her not speaking to me and all, and my wife got mad too, but not at her; at me!

"You've always told me that I need to be nicer to our neighbors," I said, somewhat confounded.

"With Mr. Winky in your hand? Really? This is your idea of being friendly? You're lucky she didn't call the police."

"The police! I know she's moody and a little peculiar, but why would she call the police? It's not like I shook it at her and said, 'Hey Baby, you want to wrestle the Danaconda?' She caught me in the middle of a natural act I was just trying to let her know that everything was okay between us. If she'd been squatting in her back yard and I saw her I'd have went over and said hello."

"I bet you would have."

"You darn tootin. I'm a nice guy. Why, I'd have strolled right over to that fence and made small talk until she finished. Pissing's a lonely business you know."

"I give up," My wife said.

Maybe someone can tell me what I did wrong here. I was in my own yard not bothering anyone. It wasn't a planned exposure. It was an accident that I tried to make the best of. I'm pretty quick on my feet. Besides I like peeing outside. It's liberating. So what if my neighbor's uppity wife got offended?

27

That's what's wrong with this country today, too many people offended for the trivial things and not enough people offended by the questionable talent represented by rap music.

So I mulled it over and realized that maybe everyone is not as free-thinking and, well...cool as I am. It's possible that I was misunderstood. I went over to apologize.

"Hidey ho neighbor." I said to old Julio when he answered the door. Me and him have always been friends despite the fact that he's always pestering me about returning some tools I borrowed about two, maybe three years ago. He stepped out on the porch and closed the door behind him. I felt a bit of tension in the air. Man, somebody needs to dump a load of Prozac in this neighborhood's water supply.

"Listen, Dan, Meg's a little funny right now so maybe you shouldn't be peeing outdoors for a while or at least try to hide it better," he said real quiet-like. I got the feeling Meggie Baby was standing just inside the door listening, hoping I'd make a smartass remark so she could spring on me and rip my eyes out like the she-devil she is. I hate to think what kind of demon spawn is going to claw its way out of that belly.

"All right, all right J-Man, I'll do better, but as soon as she drops that load I'm going to be out and about again so you'd better warn her." We shook hands and I walked back over to my place feeling pretty good about things. Not everyone is fortunate enough to have a good neighbor like me who's willing to work things out.

I thought that had pretty much settled things until I received a letter from the Homeowners Association. This is the name they go by but I know they are actually a covert Communist organization. They'd make us wear uniforms and make us eat in a mess hall if they could.

Apparently I made a mistake in trusting Julio. I realized then that me and Julio are not friends and we've never been down by the schoolyard. In reality I had only pretended he was my friend because of his good connections in the HOA and his extensive tool collection. I'm slightly terrified of him. He wants to be president so bad his nose starts running when he talks about it and I know in my heart that he'd burn my house down if I painted my shutters a color that didn't match my shingles. What he doesn't know is that through a little covert operation of my own, I know his wife's carpet doesn't match her drapes. I haven't related this to anyone else before now because I've always strived to be a gentleman.

Now because of Julio's big mouth and misguided ambition I had to do two things I don't enjoy doing, writing and lying. I sat down and wrote a letter to the HOA explaining my position:

Dear Members of the Association Board,

Apparently there was a misunderstanding with my friend and neighbor, Mr. Rodriguez. I have never in the past nor ever will in the future willingly expose myself to a pregnant woman. What would be the purpose? She's pregnant. There's nothing I can do to and for her that hasn't already been done. It's crowded enough in there as it is.

Second: I'm well aware of the stipulations drawn out in the charter of our HOA that ban urinating outdoors.

I still shudder when I think of Mr. Rheingold, God rest his soul, accidently locking himself out of his house and having to hold off peeing for so long he seized up. "My bladder was like a magnificent stone in my belly. I had to piss so bad I couldn't feel my balls," he recounted later for anyone with the heart to listen. It's a shame that no one takes the time to listen to our elderly anymore. Finally, when agony trumped modesty and he could stand it no longer he waddled over behind his garage, unleashing a torrent so loud it caught the attention of Mrs. Warren next door. Of course she turned him in because that's what HOA members do.

As you remember, poor old Al was thrown in the stocks at the front gate of our pristine community for all to see and for ill-kept boys to spit at and taunt. When he was finally released the physical toll and embarrassment was too much for his ninety-two-year-

old heart. Correct me if I'm wrong but I don't think anyone from the neighborhood went to his funeral. Maybe it served him right. Who am I to judge?

Doggone it, I hate to have to grovel here but for the sake of peace and tranquility in my small part of this fine community I'm invested heavily in, I'll say that particular incident was an error that I won't tolerate from myself and certainly will not be repeated. I hope my utter sincerity in this matter is as clear as the windows I was reminded to wash last summer even though our state was suffering a drought like we haven't seen in thirty years. I hate to cut our correspondence short but there's more than three leaves lying in my yard at the moment and I know you have people watching.

Signed: Mr. Roberts (aka The Dan)

Strangely enough, this letter elicited a response that was not only snobbish in its tone but also a little threatening. They went over everything I had already discussed, once more reminding me of my obligations to my community. You can't spell communist without community, or can you? Anyway, I promised again, sincerely that I would not pee outside again in broad daylight. I didn't say anything about taking a shit though.

For the unlucky people who aren't blessed with an HOA and aren't sure what purpose they could possibly serve, let me enlighten you. Let's say you're at the flea market and you come across a bitchin' gargoyle mailbox. It is love at first sight and as soon as you get home you put that bad boy up. You may have noticed that everyone's mailbox looked exactly the same, until now. You're a rebel, you've made a statement, and asserted your individuality.

But before you reach the safety of your up-to-code front door, a couple of head honchos from the HOA shows up. Usually, this is a woman who secretly hates sex with her husband and a man who secretly would like to have sex with her husband. They are there to smite the rebel from you, rend your cool mailbox asunder, and burn it before anyone can be offended by it. That may sound a little dramatic but things could get out of hand without their diligence.

Thanks to the untiring efforts of our Homeowner's Association we've been free of crack heads, hos (well mostly), and American flags flown on non-holidays. There has been no gang violence or terrorist threats. Everyone's lawn looks nice and uniform, by nice I mean none of them look worse than mine. There are no junk cars up on blocks, no candy-striped houses, or stripper poles on anyone's front porch. All this has sameness and tranquility been accomplished because of few hard-working people with too much time on their hands. You know who you are.

I know I'm being watched but I've got my eye out too. I know if a stripper pole does go up on someone's front porch there's a better than even chance it will be right next door. I'm betting that someday old Meg is going to get bored with life in suburbia. She'll start thinking about the glory days when men paid to see her naked. She'll miss all those drunken men with a fist full of dollars in one hand and an eight dollar beer in the other. I've been hoarding my ones in anticipation. A ruckus will be raised. That wannabe dictator, Julio, is never going to be president if I can help it. He and Meg may even have to move. When they do, out in the backyard I'll go, liberated. If I see a neighbor this time, why, I'm not even going to wave. I tried to be friendly once and where did that get me? Those of us who pee freely, pee alone.

Faux Paw

I've always wanted to own an exotic pet of some sort. An alligator maybe, a cheetah, or a chimpanzee, something unique with the potential to one day turn on me and kill my stupid ass.

That's what I want. Yes sir. To get up in the morning, work all damn day, come home, open the door, and have my pet; the one I feed and care for; who I've rescued from a shabby existence or possibly even death, jump me and rip my throat out. It's just something else to think about on the ride home. "I wonder what's for supper. Gosh, did I pay that light bill? Will today be the day I get passed through my pet's bowels?"

I stick my head in the front door, anticipating another playful evening with my Komodo dragon. "Honey," I call to my wife, "Did we remember to pay...?" I hear a sound like the engine of a muscle car thrumming to life, a blur of brown and green, a whiff of putrid breath and suddenly...*I'm* supper. "Oh God, oh my God!" I scream. My last thought on Earth is, "I should have bought a fish." What's left of me and my wife isn't found for days because two hours after the attack the power company shuts off our lights and everyone thinks we're away on vacation. We do tend to keep to ourselves.

Cute puppies, cuddly kitties, entertaining birds, and pretty fish are fine pets for some but they just don't interest me. No sir. It ups the ante and heightens the senses when you start living on the edge. Things like paying bills, wondering if Katie Holmes is really happy, and hoping we never find out Alex Trebek is an idiot without his cue cards is not even worth wasting a good worry on anymore because, dammit, I'm in a fight for my life with my pet gator.

Sure, this peril is self-imposed because I thought owning an exotic varmint would be "oh so cool". But who's going to admit they can't dominate a stupid animal? Not me. You have to let it know who's boss, that you're in control of its destiny. You can't be unnerved every time you turn suddenly to find your pet standing directly behind you, staring intently at your neck.

But it's more than just a beloved pet, it's a lifestyle. I'll bulk up with steroids and start wearing leather vests without a shirt, shave my head and get a tattoo on my face, many piercings, maybe a gold tooth. "Man, that Dan is one badass dude." My friends will say. "That may well be," their wives will reply. "But he'll never get the smell of monkey dung out of his house."

Besides the smell there are other inconveniences to sharing your couch with a creature normally seen choking the living shit out of a dik-dik. Frequent trips to the emergency room top the list. The cost may become prohibitive before I learn the proper way to disinfect cuts and abrasions, the finer points of suture, and applying plaster casts. Not only will I save time and money by administering my own first aid, it will also enhance my reputation as the "badass dude" in our ever-shrinking circle of friends. "My God, Louise, you should have been there. He re-attached his own finger, in three hours, while holding his Cheetah down with one knee. I've never anything like it." You cannot buy this type of street cred.

Strangely, some people are put off by large snakes slithering around on the family room floor or a mountain lion gently cuffing their toddlers around in the rumpus room. That's why they are so much more comfortable with a pit bull around. Personally, I love pit bulls. Who doesn't really? Who wouldn't want one of these darling little scamps in their homes, especially if they have small children?

In fairness to the dog, if someone invited me into their home where all I had to do is eat free food, nap all day, and lick myself, I'd pounce on the nearest perceived threat to that sweet set-up too. Even if it was wearing Sponge Bob PJs. Really now, what kind of jackass moron do you have to be to bring a pit bull into your home if you have a child? Unless, of course, you're not particularly fond of that child.

People say, "Oh no, they're good dogs, it's just bad people making them bad." Hmmm. Let's stop and think about that for a moment. Maybe my news comes through a different portal but I seldom if ever read or hear of a child being mauled by a Pekingese.

Pit bulls are mean sons-of-bitches, just biding their time, waiting for the perfect moment to go to their owner's ass. The owner wakes up one morning and says "Hey there Butch, what you got in your mouth there buddy?" And then it dawns in his pea-brain right before he starts screaming, "Oh my God, it's my left arm."

Now I don't mind if you own a pit bull and I don't care what you do with it in the privacy of your own home. If you want to turn it into a damn killing machine to be set loose on some unsuspecting dumbass burglar's scrotum, that is fine with me. I just don't want the bastard out running around loose in my neighborhood. I don't want the 235 pounds of force from his formidable jaws clamping down on my gluteus maximus ripping and tearing fat and muscle tissue. It's just not a fair fight.

The big chunk taken out of my ass by this dog will significantly hamper my lifestyle, the least not being limiting my choices of well-fitting pants. Also, I won't be able to sit in a chair, despite the density or firmness of its cushion, without rolling over and spilling my Cheerwine. Some hot shot orthopedic surgeon will want to attach a titanium kickstand to my coccyx to keep me upright just so he can get his name in *The New England Journal of Medicine*. My insurance won't cover this because they'll consider it cosmetic surgery. So I'll end up doing everything half-assed the rest of my life whether I want to or not. All because of some half-wit's phallic extension on a leash. Besides there's nothing cool about getting attacked by something as mundane as a dog, a species that's supposedly domesticated.

It seems there are some people who want to own an out-of-the-ordinary pet more than I do. A Mensa reject from Florida choked to death in a cockroach eating contest attempting to win a python. This saved the python the trouble of having to do it later of course, but that's not the point. To win a big cumbersome reptile, he crammed his mouth full of bugs that most people are reluctant to step on barefooted. I don't care if he had a skewed brain and even worse breath, that's a longing the best poets can't articulate. "At least he died doing something he loved." This is what his friends say down at the dark and slimy cave where they all hang out.

Okay, no more kidding around. The chances of me controlling an exotic animal long enough for either one of us to stay alive is exactly nil. My 16 pound Shih Tzu has complete run of the house and the only fish I've owned went belly up in three days, killed with kindness. Also, my journey toward proving once and for all that I'm bat shit crazy is hampered by the fact that I'm incredibly cheap. It makes me mad when a contestant on Wheel of Fortune buys a vowel. So my dream of living the life of a suburban Tarzan is just that, a dream. But what a dream it is.

The room is dark; the only light from a flickering TV. We're sitting on the couch, my chimpanzee and me, watching an Animal Planet rerun. I fold up my kickstand and lay my head in my monkey's lap. "Oh, Mathilde," I say. "I'm so glad you're not one of those vicious dogs." She grunts softly and attempts to braid my hair, gives up and rubs her knuckles across my face; sizing it up for the day she will rip it from my skull and hand to me while I dance a bloody jig, screaming "Why, for the love of God, why!?"

Danny Roberts

Right Purty Women

If you enjoy the company of women, which I mostly do, it might sound like a hoot to be out there alone in the forest with three babes. "Oh yeah, I'm definitely the man." Unfortunately, problems, gobs of them, can spring right up and whack square you in the gonads--problems that can steadily worsen.

Take Karen here, the selfless, giving woman currently in my arms. She loves the world, has more Facebook friends than three ordinary people could muster, volunteers at the homeless shelter, and rescues cats. Yep, she's a sweet, pleasant woman, quick-witted and full of life. But that certainly doesn't make her any lighter. She was cooing over a rabbit that bounded across our path (probably fleeing for his life from a large unseen predator, but I left this unsaid), wasn't watching where she was going, clumsily stepped on a tree root, and sprained her ankle. That's how I ended up carrying caring Karen.

There was much hand-wringing and cries of anguish from the girls in our party. "Karen, are you okay?"

"Should we call for help?"

"Great idea!"

"Shoot, no bars."

"Aw. Now what do we do?" The three ladies looked at me. Since I was the only man in the group, I was expected to carry the load, so to speak.

I wanted to cry out in anguish myself at this point: "I'm not toting this clumsy bitch." But I didn't because, "I'm the man." Since hopping on one foot, for what I estimated to be two miles, back to our car would be impossible for Karen, I flexed my muscles and picked her up. She stopped sniffling.

That was about fifteen minutes ago and now my "manly" arms feel like hot lead, my back is starting to spasm, and there's a cramp in my left thigh. I also currently hate these women.

I hate the way they chattered and squealed during our

36

"quiet" walk in the woods. I loathe the way they had to identify and put a name to every plant, flower, tree, leaf, and animal upon the ground, fowl in the sky, and every single, solitary, stupid damned fish swimming in the streams. I hate the way they felt compelled to take pictures of dirt.

"Karen, are you okay?" Angie asked for the umpteenth time. "You think you'll still be able to go out tonight?"

Yes sir, I thought. *My hemorrhoids will look like the tailpipe of a '67 Cadillac and I'll have a hernia that could go on display at the Smithsonian, but these gals are more worried about Karen's social life.*

"How are you doing honey?" Denise rubbed my back reassuringly.

"There's a river of sweat running down the crack of my ass, not to put too fine a point on it." I said.

Denise shot me a look. "None of this is my fault," it said.

I decided it best to change tacks. "Fine, I could do this all day." I scared up what must have been a ghastly smile and kept on carrying on.

It serves me right that I got myself into this predicament. All the useless crap I've talked about women over the years. I'll see a somewhat unattractive girl in a bar and can't resist saying something like, "If Jack Daniels don't make her pretty, Avon ain't got a chance."

Or after a long day working with a bunch of women best described as a herd, I plop down on the sofa and turn on the television to watch the news. Sure, I want to be informed, but I'm also expecting to see a lady of at least reasonable attractiveness. It makes the horror of reality go down smoother. Instead, standing there in front of the state capitol building with a microphone in her hand is a gal who needs a bell around her neck and a pasture to complete the panorama. I turn to my wife, who really is a pretty person with a kind heart, and say, "Damn, that girl is butt ass ugly."

"It's the blouse she's wearing," Denise says. "It's not flattering."

"You're right baby, if she pulled it over her head it'd look a whole lot better on her."

Why do I say these things? It's not like I have any room to talk about someone's appearance. Any looks I had Mother Nature stomped out of me years ago.

Maybe I do place too much emphasis on looks and not enough on character or intelligence. It could be. I don't know. I really don't give a flying flip at this point. This isn't the time for introspection, quiet or otherwise. I'm shallow. I've learned to live with it. Damn karma's ass.

Meanwhile, I'm plodding along at the moment with my ankles popping like the uncorking of a champagne bottle; my knees throbbing like the hangover headache that follows. I was thinking about whistling just to show off when a little voice in my head said, "Hello Dan, this is Aphrodite. All women are beautiful, you schmuck. You want to feel like the king turd, Mister Man? You think you can say all those nasty things about women and there never be any repercussions? Well think again bucko. Here's *three* women, handle them."

Man I got to set this hussy down for a second. "You ladies look like you need a rest," I said.

"No, no, we're fine." they said in unison. I wondered how long it would take authorities to locate all three bodies.

I sat Karen down and stretched my back. Angie and Denise took up a position on either side of her, holding her up, they looked like an awkward chorus line.

"How much more daylight do we have left?" Denise asked tentatively. The far off howl of a coyote answered her. The girls yipped and huddled closer together. "We need to hurry now." Denise said.

I looked at Karen's ankle. It was a nice shade of purple. She wouldn't be doing any dancing tonight. Unless hopping around on one foot trying to fend off a pack of wolves could be called dancing. That last thought made me laugh on the inside and I felt better, lighter somehow. I scooped Karen up and our little troop staggered onward.

So here's the real deal. I actually have a lot of respect for most women, even porn actresses. Hey, everybody's got to make a buck. There are some notable exceptions. Hillary Clinton and Nancy Pelosi come to mind. Porn stars aren't angels but at least they're not trying to screw the whole country. For some reason though, I've never been able to remain friends with any woman I've had a romantic relationship with. I don't know what we'd talk about unless it was how grateful they were to be rid of me. But at least we'd be talking about me and that's the important part.

I decided to tell the girls a story between wheezes because I was starting to weaken. Maybe it would help soothe their nerves and occupy my mind with something besides pain. "Did I ever tell you the story about my friend who decided to piss into the abyss?"

"No, we don't think so." they all agreed. A story no one has heard. This is what makes life worth living.

"My friend Alan went camping with some buddies and they pitched camp beside a deep ravine. Of course they all got drunk and eventually passed out. During the middle of the night, Alan woke up with a screaming bladder and, still woozy, staggered out into the dark to relieve himself. 'I'm going to take a leak into the world's largest urinal,' he must have thought, because he walked right up to the edge and whipped it out. Standing there peeing into the void he looked up at the brilliant stars and lost his balance. Trying not to fall on his ass he over-corrected and pitched forward into oblivion. He must have smacked the canyon wall a couple of times pretty hard before he landed. They found him the next morning with his arms flung over his head and something in his hand. It was his penis. He'd ripped it completely off his body. Yep, he was hanging on to that thing like a macaque clinging to a banana."

"Eww, is that true."

"Yes sir, I mean yes ma'am. It's a man's most prized possession and we still like women enough to loan it to them occasionally."

"Okay, Danny, that's enough." Denise gave me another look.

The car was in sight when a rustle came from the bushes in

front of us. A bear cub came ambling out onto the trail. I dropped Karen with a thud. She screamed and the bear scrambled back into the brush from where it came with a mew-like cry. Denise and Angie lifted Karen up on her good ankle and, calling me names, helped her hop towards the car.

Suddenly there was a bigger thrashing from the undergrowth directly behind me. I turned to face a very large mama bear. I took off running in the direction of the car. I passed the girls and yelled, "Everyone for themselves!" I no longer felt like "The Man."

Mama bear ran past them as they stood frozen in place. I was reaching for the door handle when the bear knocked me down. I screamed and thrashed about as she grabbed my ankle in her mouth. "Dan," I heard another little voice say as the bear dragged me into the woods. "This is Artemis. It looks as if you have your hands full with another female. She's magnificent isn't she?"

"But I love women!" I screamed, much like a girl, right before mama bear's mouth closed over my head and I settled into peaceful darkness.

Alex the Dog

Men are dogs. My wife reminds me of this when a Victoria's Secret commercial on TV stops me dead in my tracks. "I thought you had to go to the bathroom," she says.

"I can hold it," I answer. What's another thirty unnecessary seconds of agony?

"Men are dogs," she says with disgust.

That may be but if I had to be an animal of the four-legged variety, dogs would be my pick. Especially my dog. That little SOB has it made.

You've seen the bumper stickers, "My rescue dog rescued me." That's not exactly how it happened at my house. We weren't rescued we were brainwashed.

The first time I met Alex the Dog my first question was, "What is it?"

"It's a Shih-Tzu." Denise said. "He's officially a dog, with papers, for fifteen dollars we got a bargain." But in some cases you truly get what you pay for.

Initially, Alex couldn't make up his mind right away whether we would be a good fit or not. After making a careful inspection of our house, judging whether it met the criteria of a dog of his stature, he finally decided we would probably be okay to live with, for a little while anyway. He still had his fancy digs at the pound to go back to, no matter how temporary, and he wanted us to be aware of that. We were so grateful that he decided to stay we gave him full run of the house.

This wasn't our initial plan of course. We both had huge aspirations of being his master. We would teach our new dog to sit, stay, come, and not bring blood from my mother-in-law's fingers when she tried to give him a treat. That last one was Denise's idea but I went along with it too.

Alex did eventually learn all of these commands but at his own leisure and at different degrees than we had hoped for. He "sat" and "stayed" where, when, and as long as he liked. He "came" only when he heard his dinner dish being filled or when we held something in our hands that looked vaguely interesting from a distance. He stopped gnawing on Denise's mother's fingers once she started leaving his treats on the floor and kept her hands in her pockets.

Overall I think the training went fairly well.

Fearful Alex would become bored with us, we purchased every dog toy imaginable. Most of which remain ignored while he plays with empty water bottles. The big exception is the toy that squeaks when he chews it, yes he certainly loves that one. It's his favorite. In every room at every hour of the day he loves it, without respite. I can hear it at this very moment.

Wanting our cute little dog to sleep well, we bought him a bed that looked a whole lot more comfortable than the one we sleep in. He likes his bed so much that he sleeps in ours every night, curled up on our feet or draped across our heads. "Tonight," we say, putting our foot down. "Tonight he sleeps in his own bed." We tried all manner of tactics to accomplish this. We pointed to his bed, identifying it for him. "This is Alex's bed." He looked at it and looked at us, "So?" he seemed to say. We pleaded and used pantomime to show him where and how he was to sleep. To an outside observer we would have looked like a couple suffering a complete and severe nervous breakdown.

"Alex, get down!" is the stern command heard at all hours of the night as we lie awake daydreaming of the sleep we used to enjoy. He takes this to mean reposition himself in a more comfortable spot without actually having to get off the bed. But we're not going to waver. We mean it, someday he will sleep in his own bed. Probably not tonight though.

So this was a true breed of dog with papers? I got excited about this, thinking "show dog" and possibly "prize money". I don't know how this dog show racket works but by my reckoning there had to be some kind of monetary gain. Why else would people go through all that time and trouble to train a dog for show? Not that there is a lot of training needed. I've watched the Westminster and all the dogs have do is look pretty and prance around in front of an audience, obey a few simple commands, and nibble a morsel of food occasionally. Not unlike your basic supermodel. Alex had other plans though. Apparently he doesn't like his mouth checked and his butt held in the Westminster style of dog showing. Although checking out his own butt *with* his mouth is an activity he enjoys immensely.

As time passed I realized Alex the Dog had no interest in learning any tricks or obeying any basic commands. Neither of us had the desire or patience to further our master-dog relationship. I was exhausted and he was annoyed. We'd reached a stalemate. "I think it's possible that he's just stupid." I told my wife.

One day I pulled out those vaunted papers of his to possibly get some insight on this animal that currently ran my house. He was one and a half years old and had had two previous owners, already. We were his third owner. At the pace he was setting he would go through twenty-eight owners in his lifetime, and that's not in dog years. That's a tremendous amount of "rescued people".

"Well, clearly the problem isn't me. He's neurotic," I said to myself. I looked over the top of the papers in my hand and there stood Alex the Dog staring at me. "What are you doing man?" He seemed to be thinking. "You doing a background check? You might not like what you find... master."

He changed then, but I'm not sure if it was for the better. On his own he just kind of drifted into sitting up and begging, fetching and letting us know when he needed to go out. It was like he was saying, "I can do any number of things, when I choose to." We were so overjoyed that our dog wasn't retarded after all, that we started rewarding him lavishly for the least little thing. "Look he pooped on the tile instead of the carpet, give him a good-boy cookie." He did so little to receive so much he could have been a member of Congress.

Have you ever been in a bad relationship with an extremely attractive person? Me neither, but I've heard about them.

Apparently you get walked on because they're just so darn good-looking. They string you along, giving you just enough to keep you hanging on and hoping they may one day care for you. Deep in your heart you know they could care less. That's my dog.

He's playful, fun, and loving one minute, the sweetest little fuzzy puppy in the whole world. Then, for reasons only known to him, he seems intent on maiming one of us. Denise claims he's bipolar. He hasn't done any serious damage yet because he only weighs seventeen pounds. It's nerve-racking living with a time bomb. I've given thought to sending him and his squeaky toy packing but that would feel too much like he had won after all. I can't be defeated by a borderline imbecile, besides he's just so darn cute.

Sometimes, when Alex is licking himself on some intriguing area of his body, Denise will yell at him, "Alex, stop it that's disgusting!" Then, because I'm the other dog in the house, she turns on me. "He's definitely your dog because he acts just like you." This is mostly unfair; unfair to voice it, not the assessment because secretly I'm thinking, "You know for a man to get licked there he would have to be in a committed relationship with an adventurous partner or be willing to cough up some serious dough." This is probably the way a canine would think so I guess my wife is right. I ain't nothing but a hound dog. I just don't have all the perks of Alex. Lucky dog.

We're Flush!

It's sad really, what we've latched onto at work to brighten our days. But with no pay increases for going on five years, the 401-K exterminated, and ever-increasing health insurance premiums, we've all begun to understand the importance of little things. As Voltaire said, "Life is a shipwreck but we must not forget to sing in the lifeboats." Which in my neck of the woods means, "The sun doesn't shine on the same dog's ass every day." Or not. The point being is, today we were gifted with a new toilet in our bathroom and there are smiles all around.

The American buttocks is not as refined as the French derriere, so although it's not as sophisticated as a bidet, shooting a stream of water up your crack, it's still pretty tricked-out as toilets go. First thing you notice is how shiny, clean, and stain-free it is, for the time being anyway. You almost feel a pang of guilt soiling it. It's also a good two inches taller than the old unit, allowing you to lower yourself down easier and quicker. This is mighty important if you're cramping like a bitch and speaking in tongues when you arrive there. Hauling your carcass back up is a lot less taxing, too, if you're weak or tired from exertion.

But none of that compares to the flushing action. I've never seen 1.6 gallons of water disappear so fast in my entire life. I barely touched the handle, there was a giant sucking sound, and whoosh! That baby was out of there. There wasn't even time to check for any unusual colorings or objects in your handiwork. The only thing I can compare it to is the mass exodus of humanity tearing out the door at quitting time on Fridays.

I asked Anne, our dispatcher, if she had had a chance to give our newest company expenditure a whirl. Normally I don't speak to members of the opposite sex about bathroom visits, but dammit, this was impressive. "You better not drop an earring or anything else you might want to retrieve in that bowl, because when you touch that handle it ain't coming back. Why, you could stick your foot in there and flush and it would rip your shoe right off."

I wasn't suggesting she try that of course. Although the image of her limping back into the office with one bare, wet foot was pretty damn funny it would also be a tragedy of sorts. To a woman losing a shoe is worse than losing a kitten…or a tooth.

We have enough crying around there as it is.

The old toilet will be missed; the way you miss a disagreeable aunt who pinched you hard because you were her favorite. Sometimes the old flusher would just start running and not stop for any discernible reason; the toilet, not the aunt. Other times, the toilet regurgitated your offering up and over the rim and onto the floor and down the hall. There's nothing like tiptoeing around a turd that may or may not be yours on the way to the break room to grab a snack. It put some people off their feed, but not me. I'm a eater.

This caused management to fret, wring their hands, and call hasty meetings, to weigh their options.

"Gosh, the water bill shot up a whole seventy-nine cents last month!"

"Good God man!"

"Yes. But compare that against the price of replacing the old unit. I think we need to stand pat for now. Now let's discuss that chewing gum on the sidewalk. Anyone have suggestions?"

But all of that nonsense came to an end when Arturo, the man in charge of our building's maintenance, walked in sweating and cussing under the weight of a large carton. He mumbled something about how ungrateful we all were. We knew he was in a good mood because he's happiest when he can piss and moan while he works. It's ironic that Arturo would be the bearer of good things. I don't think he has purposely made anyone smile in his entire life. He resembles a large garden gnome and I'm sure mothers use him to scare their children. "You better eat your peas, Gretchen, or Arturo will come and get you." Cruel yes, but also effective.

We lowly worker bees are not trying to be greedy here, but now that the exit fluids have been taken care of something needs to be done about our intake. The ungracious bastards we are, we now are petitioning for a water fountain. The nerve. The only solution available now is to lug in jugs of drinking water and store them in our refrigerator already filled with many mysterious items. Some of them edible. If you forget to bring water that day well tough noogies cowboy, it's a rough world out here. How nice it would be to stroll up to a water fountain, simply push a button, and voila, out comes clear, cool water to drink. It would feel like we had finally arrived, so…cosmopolitan.

I know I'm a dreamer, but someday I envision a sink in our break/storage/chair assembly room. The only sink we have now is beside the new supersonic toilet. You bring leftovers from home in handy Tupperware bowls and after finishing up your Hamburger Helper cheesy macaroni there's nowhere to clean them except in the same sink where someone has (hopefully) washed their hands after doing God knows what not two feet away. I'm not fastidious, but even a puny little germ can kick your ass. My wife warned me that the next time I come home with crusty dishes, she's never fixing my lunch again. A quandary, but I think I may have a solution. Unless a new sink arrives before I retire or die I think I could plunge my empty bowls down in the new speedy toilet. I know it sounds pretty gross, but at the speed at which this thing moves water, there can't possibly be any germs tough enough to survive this onslaught. The force would rip any stubborn food particles off and, if I wasn't careful, the dish right out of my hand. I would need to use both hands which would require an assistant to push the handle. This is teamwork at its highest level. It may even get us a mention in the company newsletter.

My Town

Okay, what do you have to do to get a town named after you? Besides show up early I mean. A couple a hundred years ago all a brave-hearted American had to do was migrate to uncharted territory, find a parcel of land they coveted, and then claim it. There might have been a few of those pesky Native Americans living there already, protesting that it was their land, but who cared about them? Might makes right and besides they were too proud a people to lawyer up.

After the land was cleared, trees felled, rivers fouled, game slaughtered for sport, and everything else set to rights, it was time to build a town. Up went a saloon, a church, a mercantile, and a whorehouse where people could drink, worship, mercantile, and ... dicker. Civilization is a beautiful thing.

One day a squinty-eyed settler, back straight, chin held high, stood on the outskirts of his new metropolis, admiring his creation and pondering opening up a bank, when another traveler of the new frontier pulled up in his Conestoga.

"Howdy Brig, this sure is a fine town you got here."

"Well Frank, the more I look at it the more I have to agree. You know, I don't want to brag but I did do all the planning and the layout of this here municipality myself."

"Yep, I have to admit, Brig, I've never seen four buildings arranged in a better square. So what you fixin' to call it?"

"Well Frank. Since I led the party out here and did most of the work I thought it only fitting that I name it after me."

"Brigham? Youngstown? Those are as good a name as any for a town."

"Nope, I'm gonna call it Brighamville."

"That sounds mighty fine."

Nowadays, starting a town from scratch seems like a lot more work than the average person could muster. Even worse you have to do something remarkably spectacular to get an existing town to change its name in your honor. I'm thinking of you Joe, Montana. Since my chances of becoming a Hall-of-Fame-Quarterback with the last name of a state are pretty darn slim, I considered lowering my sights temporarily. Maybe I would opt for a street, a building, or, if all else failed, a bridge.

I recently visited a town named for a hero from the Revolutionary War. Yeah, like who remembers that? While in this city I crossed the Billy "Crash" Craddock Bridge. I'm sorry Mr. Craddock (may I call you Crash?) but I have no idea who in the hell you are. Apparently they'll name a bridge after anybody. That might be a good place for me to start, without losing my dream of a town, of course.

The Danny R. Roberts Bridge. If you say it real fast, it doesn't sound half bad. There will be some people, some *small* people, who will be jealous and say, "I don't know who in the hell Danny R. Roberts is. Why does he get a bridge named after him?" Then some official will have to explain, "Well, he did camp out down here six weeks before the bridge was completed and he was the first one to cross it. We had to name it something and gosh, he looked so pitiful and all."

"What about Horse Piddle Creek Bridge? The creek's been there longer than this yahoo and people have at least heard of the creek."

"Well, yeah, I guess there's that."

Up to that point it will be the proudest moment of my life. Since it will be my bridge, I'll let people fish off it and spit over the side. It'll be a friendly, blue-collar bridge, not like that snooty one out in San Francisco. Of course after a couple of weeks the new will wear off and I'll start thinking of my own town again.

For me to do something remarkably spectacular, a heavy technological miracle would have to take place, a grand experiment for the betterment of all, even people who don't deserve it. Something like the first manned flight to Uranus. A volunteer will be needed, a brave patriot who will put the good of mankind ahead of any regard for his own safety, a complete idiot, me. I've been thinking about this for a while, you know. Strap my ass in a rocket and fire me off into space. I'll be gone

49

ten years or so but when I get back, boy, will I live the high life.

I once struck up a conversation with a pretty girl in a bar and we'd actually gotten along well enough to talk about dreams and aspirations. The fact that I was buying her a steady stream of tequila shots didn't hurt. After telling me about her dreams of being a singer/actress she asked about my goals.

"Well," I said, "Someday, I'd really like to be the first man on Uranus." She threw her drink in my face, slapped me, and went to complain to the manager. I think I may have pronounced it wrong.

Since then, of course, I have learned how stupid it was to say that to her. Uranus is just a big ball of gas, much like our President, and you can't actually land on it. But I could circle it a couple of times and head on home. That's an awfully long way to travel just to look at something, but I know people who have driven all the way to Niagara Falls just for that very same reason.

With my luck, the day I return to Earth will be the same day a new I-Phone debuts or Kibbles the Kardashian Kat has her new movie premiere. I'll be mostly ignored, relegated to the odd news at the end of the broadcast, up there with "Man teaches pet monkey to be designated driver."

A Mayor of some small town will offer me a key to their city and, I got to tell ya, if this is all I get for all my hard work I'm going to be one pissed off, grubby science experiment. "No, Hell no, I don't want a key! I want my own TOWN!" I get a little cranky from long trips sometimes.

If I have to I'll take my case to the most powerful person on Earth, Oprah. She'll sit me on her couch and say, "Tell me about Uranus." I'll chuckle and nod knowingly. "There's a lot of gas Oprah, a lot, you have to be careful how you approach it."

The big problem is, even if the back-stabbing bastards officially known as the U.S. Government finally relent and give me my own town, I won't know what to name it. There's a Danville right up the road in Virginia. I've been there and it's just not that impressive. Robertsville is too staid. Dannytown sounds like a store at the mall where metrosexuals buy their duds. People will try to rhyme Danboro with dingle berry and laugh cruelly. Maybe I'll just call it The City of Dan. That has some old world charm to it, like the Firth of Forth or Filch a Fifth.

"Where you headed off to, Chester?"

"I'm visiting The City of Dan."

"Why are you going to that dump on a Saturday night?"

"To visit the mercantile ... yeah that's it, the mercantile. They have some new goods there, I hear."

"Well, you might want to strap on a little protection before you examine them new 'goods'.

So getting that town I covet will require most of my attention and care to keep out the riff-raff. I'll have to be on guard to make sure it always measures up to the standards I expect from a town carrying my name. I'll need to work tirelessly, 24/7, 365 or else it may become a joke. Come to think of it that sounds like a pain in the ass. I'd be just as proud to have a plaque on a bridge and I wouldn't have to circle Uranus.

Danny Roberts

The Allergic Slide

It started with a slow death march up and down the aisles of Hobby Lobby. Denise was searching for that perfect item; one that I could carry to the car and into our home, hang on three different walls at four different heights, and she could admire it for a whole day. After twenty-four hours she would then forget this perfect item ever existed. I was promised a milkshake if I came along peaceably. After twenty-two years of marriage, these are the kinds of deals you make.

I was really getting down on that Snickers double chocolate milkshake, when my tongue started feeling odd. It should have been humming Zip-a-Dee-Doo-Dah all the live long day, or however the hell that song goes, not getting all out of sorts. It felt like I had a mouth full of lard. "Honey," I garbled. "I tink sumpin is wong wih my ton." I stuck it out. It was big; a colossal wonder of the world, maybe a genuine eighth.

"Oh my God" She screamed, and did a quick, neat U-turn right in the middle of a busy four-lane street, speeding me off to the doctor. Barely missing two cars and a truck, and running an ice cream truck into the ditch, we caused much consternation amongst the other drivers. They reacted accordingly with squealing tires, blasting horns, and creative hand gestures. Something about being behind the wheel of a car spurs people's imagination.

Despite this hubbub I had a moment to reflect. My tongue had gotten me in trouble before but it was usually something the brain started. "Hey, that would be funny as hell," My brain would spark. And since my tongue has absolutely no self-control, out that idea came. That idea never sounded as good out in the open air. But this time my tongue had turned on me without provocation. This was something new, to ponder, and possibly enter into a journal.

We arrived at the doctor and, though I'm a new patient there, they saw me right away, rushing me ahead of snot-slinging children and elderly people wobbling on canes. "Having patients die in the lobby is bad for business" was Denise's theory for their haste. I thought this to be fairly accurate. Once more I

had to unfurl the tongue, to a complete stranger, a nurse named Amanda.

Nurse Amanda appeared to be in her mid to late thirties, efficient and professional; I was thinking she had seen a lot worse things come through that door than what I had to offer. I was in the presence of compassion, in gentle and healing hands.

"Oh my God!" She screamed when my tongue flopped out at her, weaving like a charmed cobra. "What the hell is it?"

Not exactly the soothing words I was hoping for.

Can you still breathe and swallow okay?" She finally asked.

"Yeth." I said, and nodded vigorously in case she misunderstood.

"I'll send the doctor in right away." Not quite running, Nurse Amanda made for the door.

I sat on the edge of the table, swinging my legs and contemplating my plight. As last meals go, a double chocolate Snickers milkshake is not too shabby. I didn't really think that would be my last meal, but then again most people don't get up from the table, pat their belly, and say, "Hey that was my last meal." There are exceptions of course, if they're getting ready to eat a bullet maybe, or have a date with the hangman, they can make that bold statement with a cocky flair. But since I was in the capable hands of the best health care providers my insurance would cover I felt fairly confident I would be eating again. It could be through a straw or intravenously but hey, a meal's a meal.

A young doctor swaggered in, exuding the kind confidence only people full of life and with normal-sized tongues can portray. He told me his name was Chase, which was slightly disturbing because that's not a name it's an activity. I shook his hand and said "unth".

"Open up and say "aah." He said. "Let's see what we've got here." He grabbed my tongue with both hands. "Yep, that's a nice one alright." He sounded like he was grading a cantaloupe. Still, it was good to get a professional opinion. "So are you on any medications?" Denise gave him a complete rundown in alphabetical order. Trust me this woman never forgets anything. Dr. Chase rubbed his chin and said "Hmmm." A very educated "hmmm" it sounded like. I started to relax. "Have you been stung, bitten, or gored by an Ibex lately?"

"Wha you me by watewy?"

Denise stepped up and took charge, she's used to explaining me to people anyway so this was her time to shine. "Well this morning he took an Ibuprofen for his back and I guess that's why his tongue looks like it belongs in a yak. A couple of months ago he took one of my prescription pills, Diclofenac, probably not the smartest thing in the world to do but, hey, he's experimented with drugs before. His jaw swelled up like there was a big chaw of tobacco in there, but since that's the only disgusting habit he doesn't have I figured it was the drug, again."

"Hmmm..." Dr. Chase held up his finger. "So he's had swelling in his jaw and his tongue. I'm guessing now, but is this unusual?"

"Well," Denise said. "His head does get bigger every year but it has always been in small increments, not all at once like this."

"Hello, I'm sitting right here." I wanted to say, but since I couldn't actually talk I decided not to say anything.

"But this is nothing compared to the first time." Denise went on. "You should have been there for that freak show. That was caused by something called Septra."

"Septra?"

"I know it sounds like a giant lizard from a Japanese movie but it's actually a tiny little pill."

The young doctor looked a little testy. "I know what Septra is."

I had to believe that Denise would not have been quite so flip if it was her tongue being wrangled like an unruly steer.

"Anyway, this was prescribed by a "doctor" who

apparently won her medical license in a raffle at the Elks lodge. A complete idiot. I wake up at three in the morning from the best sleep I've had in months and the Elephant Man is standing in my bathroom."

"So you've had trouble sleeping?"

"Well, yes," Denise continued. "I wake up three or four times a night most nights. Gosh, sometimes I just get so tired."

"I bet." Doctor Chase seemed genuinely concerned for the first time since we arrived. "What we could do..."

"Unth!" I said and they turned back to me with more than a little irritation.

"Sooo..." Demise continued. "While Danny's sitting in the examining room at ER every employee on third shift, including a guy with a mop and a bucket, stuck their head in to see if "he was okay". They weren't that concerned for his health, they just wanted to see that freak in room number three. Danny kept saying, "I'm not an animal." Over and over. It was pretty embarrassing. Surprisingly no one took pictures though I did offer."

"So, you've had three different episodes shortly after taking medication?" The confident, young doctor turned to me, apparently thinking Denise's sleep problems could be charged on a separate bill.

"Uh-huh."

"Well, I think it's safe to say you're allergic to sulfa, penicillin, and Nsaids. Nsaids is Non-steroidal anti-inflammatory drugs. No aspirin, no ibuprofen, Aleve, or Advil for you."

Wow, now that was a damn diagnosis if I ever heard one. I was allergic to penicillin, sulfa, and that Nsaids thing. Apparently everything that could help keep me alive could also kill me. I think I felt chagrined.

"You can still take Tylenol of course."

Ah Tylenol, the most trusted name in over-the-counter medication, except for that little cyanide incident back in 1982.

"I'll send someone to give you a steroid shot and you should be fine." Dr. Chase swaggered out with the confidence only people who know they're not getting a needle stuck in them can exude.

They sent a different nurse in to give me my shot. Nurse Amanda was in the employee break room crying uncontrollably. I started rolling up my sleeve "Huh-uh," The new health care professional said. "This one goes in your butt." Apparently she wanted my face as far away from her as possible.

A couple of days later a friend called to inquire about my health. "What the Hell is wrong with you?" He's asked me this same question many times before.

"Well, it's like this. I'm allergic to penicillin, sulfa, and something called Nsaids."

"Incest!"

"Yes, can you believe it? Here I've been enjoying it for years and now I'm allergic to it. I guess those country roads won't be taking me home anytime soon."

According to what we see advertised on TV there are at least three drugs for every ailment imaginable, especially in my age group. Erectile dysfunction, hair loss, over-active bladder, memory loss, depression, unable to budge on social issues, aversion to new music, the list just goes on and on. There are some problems I didn't even know I had. But what scares me, especially now, are the side effects of the cures. Boy, did I used to have fun scoffing at those commercials? The announcer in a low and impossibly quick voice telling us we may experience anal bleeding, blurred vision, finger nails falling out, numbness in scrotum, neck may turn black and/or blue, maniacal laughing, dandruff, bestiality, heart exploding, hallucinations, speaking in tongues, and an uncontrolled urge to write everything down. But these things aren't funny anymore. No sir.

The next time I wake up with a screaming hangover and there's no Tylenol in the medicine cabinet there's going to have to be a choice made. Oh God, I know I'm dying here but do I take the Ibuprofen and die a fast death or lie on the couch and die all day?" What would you do Dr. Oz?

Now That's Funny

One night down at the Pelican Bar on Ocracoke Island, we were slowly joshing our way toward the exit, feeling, I must confess, no pain. My wife was deep in animated conversation about something, probably shoes, with three or four other women of similar enthusiasm. I, meanwhile, waited patiently nearby, humming "Night Moves" and smiling up at a star-filled sky. I noticed a gentleman also waiting patiently and I figured, rightly, that his woman had been caught up in the gravitational pull formed when a group of women are discussing shopping.

Though he was a fine specimen, the very essence, of a clodhopper there was no need for him to stand alone twiddling his thumbs. "Howdy partner," I said. "It looks like these gals are going to be awhile. Would you like maybe to hear a joke?"

"Why, shore I would," he said. Just like that. "I shore would."

I took this as a yes and all systems go so I racked my brain for the dirtiest, filthiest, nastiest joke I know...and I told it to him. Then I laughed my ass off. Heh heh, Lord have mercy. He didn't even crack a smile, leading me to believe my delivery was somewhat flawed. But no...this man of high moral character was offended. He looked me right in the eye and said, "Mister, I don't appreciate that joke." The guy wasn't Jewish, Black, Chinese, or gay, I don't think, and besides the joke wasn't about any of these people, why was he offended?

I still think about that incident sometimes and wonder if that joke hit a little too close to home. It's hard to imagine it was the material alone that offended him. But who knows really?

Now I don't like to brag. I'm not any good at it and I sound stupid when I try. But I can tell a damn good joke. I've always wanted to tell a joke or story or maybe just write something that made someone have a physical reaction besides just a laugh. Laughing is good but I'd like to take it up a notch.

If someone told me that something they read on my website caused them to spew coffee on their computer screen that'd make me happy. Pissing their pants is good, and I'd like it if they were still wearing those same pants when they told me about it. I don't know why that's important, it just is. Shitting their pants would be a whole lot better, especially if it was so bad they had to burn those pants later. Getting choked until they had to be rescued by a stranger applying the Heimlich maneuver is getting closer to what I'm looking for.

If someone laughed so hard they threw their back out or pulled a muscle in their throat or, I know this sounds terrible, had an aneurysm or heart attack, that would mean a lot to me. It really would. I'd feel bad of course you know, but a small part of me would be going, "Damn, now that was funny." I've still got that pissed off guy to my credit and that counts for something but it's just not the same.

My dream, and I do have one, is to go to Paris. I don't care about seeing the Eiffel Tower or the Louvre and I don't care anything about eating snails or any of their other snooty little foods, but I do want to sit at one of their sidewalk cafes. I'll strike up a conversation with a pretty French girl until her boyfriend comes over and says something like "Monsieur, you American pig, you are making a mockery of yourself by speaking to Mademoiselle. If you persist I must bludgeon you."

"Now hold on there Frenchy," I'll say. "We can be friends. Sit down over there and lets me and you jaw a bit." Then I'll tell him the same joke I told on Ocracoke. Of course he'll enjoy it because he's French and they love sick shit like that. As a matter of fact, he'll laugh so hard he'll get choked on the baguette he just crammed in his mouth. Leaping to his feet and turning purple and clutching his throat, he'll tip his chair over and drag fine china and stemware crashing to the floor. Then he'll stagger into the street where he'll be flattened by a Citroen. His beret, no longer perched on a sassy French noggin, will then fly through the air landing romantically at his girlfriend's feet; in Paris everything is more romantic.

She then runs to him, kneeling at his side, afraid to touch

him because there is a lot of blood and she doesn't want to get any on her expensive designer dress. Also, he's in a hell of a lot of pain. I get up from my chair, toast him with the last of my wine and say, "C'est drole comme l'enfer n'est-ce pas?" In my dream I only speak this one line in French because it is all I need. Why get all encumbered with details?

After comforting the French lass in a good old American way that makes her ponder dual citizenship, I fly back to a real country and the best state in that country, here. I again visit Ocracoke Island and find myself, not surprisingly at The Pelican Bar where my surly friend is still wearing those same brogans and that same frown. Undeterred I stroll over to him because my mission in life is to turn that frown upside down.

"Hello there fellow bumpkin," I say. "Mister, you may not have appreciated that joke but I want you to know that it knocked 'em dead over in France."

At Least Next Week I'm on Vacation

(September 3rd)

It's not every day that you set your face on fire and then try to put it out with a pane of glass. Unless you're one of those performance artists with a few uneasy admirers and no friends. I wasn't trying to make an artistic statement about man's conflict with self-loathing and escapism, or some nonsense like that. I just wanted to get the yard mowed. Understanding your average 4-cycle Briggs and Stratton lawn mower motor isn't quantum physics, but it might as well be to my incompetent ass.

I called up a friend who has knowledge of engines both large and small and I said to him, "Why yes, it certainly does have gas in it, thank you." He then instructed me on the delicate balance of something called a carburetor and how the piston compresses the air on the up-stroke just as the spark-plug fires. He said a bunch of other stuff I didn't give a damn about as he tried to walk me through fixing that blessed little engine that was obviously smarter than me. After about forty-five minutes I was sweating like Britney Spears taking an IQ test and my hands and arms were soaked in gasoline.

The engine still wasn't working because now it was in parts, several of them, scattered about the yard, some still at arm's length, others as far away as I could throw them. Rubbing my hands across my beard, deep in thought, I pondered my next move. I didn't notice the smell of gasoline because that was all I'd been smelling for the better part of an hour.

Exhausted, I thanked my friend for his time and trouble, hung up the phone, and got myself a beer. As I sat on the patio looking at all that thick, lush grass that needed mowing before the big cook-out on Saturday, I remembered I had a Cuban cigar stashed away. Actually it was only a tiny stub, all that was left of a Cuban my father-in-law had presented to me. The old bastard had actually given me something besides a hard time for a change. I never have, and most likely never will again, enjoyed a cigar as fine as this so I wasn't wasting a bit of its precious tobacco.

Unable to focus my eyes on the tip of the cigar, even with my perfectly corrected vision, I stepped up close to the back door window and used the reflection to guide the match. There was a "whooshing" sound, the smell of burning hair and what it must look like to get a glimpse of Hell. The pain was tremendous. Not remembering to drop and roll on my face, I did what anyone would do who is temporarily out of their friggin' mind. I slammed my face into the window of the back door. Again, the pain was tremendous but at least the fire was out.

The noise brought my wife running and she had herself a good start when she saw a burned and bleeding face sticking through her back door. "Oh my God!" she yelled. "Danny, is that you?" I honestly can't think of who else it might've been.

"You betcha sweetheart, now I think it's time to take me to the hospital."

Despite my face being unusually pink in places, my eyebrows gone, and a few cuts and scrapes I thought I came out looking pretty darn good for an imbecile. When we arrived home, I was reminded that despite the excitement from earlier today, that damn yard still needed to be mowed. But I stayed upbeat because next week I'm on vacation.

(September 4th)

Over the years I've compiled a list of helpful hints to maybe get me through to another day. Most of these were written down right after I'd done something incredibly stupid. It's a fairly long list. Today I have a new addition: "Never, and I do mean never ever, take more medication than the prescription calls for." You wouldn't think this would be something I'd need to write down, but trust me, I can be forgetful.

I took an extra Percocet when I got home from the hospital last night, "just to be safe", and it knocked my ass for a loop. I slept for fourteen hours straight in a mostly dreamless, untroubled sleep. Right before I woke up, though, I dreamed I was standing in line at a medical clinic in Stockholm waiting for my new face transplant. I had picked out Robert Redford's in his Butch Cassidy and Sundance Kid days and was feeling pretty giddy, as giddy as someone could feel in a semi-comatose state anyway.

My wife finally came to check on me around eleven o'clock, "to see if I was still alive". Fortunately, I was.

Despite the fact that I didn't know what day it was, my mouth tasting like I had licked the inside of a cat litter box, and my head feeling like it was pumped up with helium, I was in good spirits. "You know what I'm going to do?" I said to her.

"Uhh...Hopefully brush your teeth?"

"Eventually, but first I'm going to get that yard mowed." I don't set my mind to something very often but when I do it takes more than a little head trauma to throw me off track.

"Are you going to hire someone?"

"No way, Jose. I'm going to sashay across that street and borrow Bob's slick green and yellow rider."

"His name is Bill and I really don't think that's a good idea."

"Bill, huh? So that's why he's been ignoring me for seventeen years."

Well I put on a hat and the biggest pair of sunglasses I own and started walking across the street to visit the newly re-named Bill. Every step I took toward his house seemed to take me farther away, like a desert oasis. Strange. I remember his house being much closer. Even stranger, I kept hearing someone call my name like they were at the bottom of a well or over a hill. I looked around but there was nobody there.

Finally reaching Bill's porch I extended my suddenly

abnormally long finger and rang his doorbell. I was staring at my fingers in wonder when Bill materialized. "Howdy...Bill." I said. Good, good, I got it right the first time.

"Hello buddy," he said. "Is there something I can do for you?"

Buddy, huh? So he didn't know my name either and apparently neither did his wife. Advantage me. "Actually there is. You may have heard about my little accident yesterday. Hell, you might have heard the commotion yourself what with me screaming and all. Anyway, bottom line is I'd like to borrow that sweet Deere John mower of yours sitting in your garage. Can you help a neighbor out?"

"Shouldn't you just go buy another mower?"

"Plan to, plan to, but if you take a gander at me you'll see I'm in no condition to be pushing a mower around right now and to be honest with you I don't have the money for a riding mower after that emergency room visit yesterday."

"You do look pretty messed up. Well, all right I guess it'll be okay but I need you to do something for me."

"I'll do what I can friend."

"Well," he said, scratching the back of his head. "Do you know anything about computers?"

"After seventeen years, I can't believe you could ask me that question, Bill," I said. "Why sure I do. Absolutely." I don't know a damn thing about computers. My reasoning was if he was asking me for computer advice he had to know less I did so maybe I could go in, punch a few buttons and, by some miracle, his old HP would be back in business. Besides I'd feel better about borrowing that sleek new mower if I did something for him in return. Not for the sake of my conscience, I'm still not sure if I have one, but if I do something good today maybe I can borrow something else of his in the future. It tied together in a neat little string of events. Something I did yesterday affects what I do today and will affect what I do tomorrow. I'm not sure if I said this last part out loud or not but Bill/Bob sure was looking at me funny. I may have been rambling, I don't know.

"Well come on in then," he said. "Come on in."

After a long walk across his living room that seemed to take days, I was finally seated in front of his computer where I tapped a few keys with my ET fingers. "What's it doing?" I asked.

"Well, sometimes it just freezes up and I can't retrieve any data I've entered."

"Well, that sounds fairly simple," I lied. "It could be a breach of the lesser Antilles which won't allow any sub-human forms of retribution to multiply overtly." I heard my friend Steve, or was it Spock, say something similar to this once and I figured, "What the hell," let's see how it sounds.

"Is that serious?"

"No, not at all. Just give me a few minutes." I started pounding keys and clicking icons like a madman. Suddenly the screen went black, then blue, and then pictures started downloading. When I say pictures I don't mean cute pictures of their children or the family dog. It was more like the family kitty, Mrs. Bill's kitty to be exact. There she was in all her glory, naked as a jaybird, reclining on her back with her legs spread.

"Oh my God!" Bill screamed, lunging for the keyboard.

"Wow, she really is a redhead," I observed.

"Shut it off, you pervert!"

Another picture came up, this time she was on all fours. "Now that's some great camera work, Bill." I said. "Look at the tits on that bitch."

"That's my bitch!" Bill sputtered. "No, that's not what I meant.

"I know what you meant neighbor, I certainly do, and you should be proud. She's a fine looking woman."

"Get out! Get out of my house!"

"Does this mean I don't get the mower?"

Bill hustled me to the front door and threw me into the yard. I flew through the air for what seemed like, again, a very long time but the landing was extremely quick, and hard. "This is a very multifaceted experience," I thought briefly before

64

agony ratcheted from my ankle to my knee. I limped back across the street and my wife met me at the door.

"What happened this time?" she asked.

"Well honey, apparently Bill's computer has a glitch so he decided to sprain my ankle. I realize this is perplexing and somewhat confusing to you." I iced down my ankle and sat on my front porch staring at the yard, watching the grass grow, and dreaming about Jamaica.

(September 5th)

I was thinking about a David Blaine card trick when I knocked the old lady's walker out of her hand. I slammed on the brakes and looked in the rearview mirror. She was bobbing forth and back, forth and back, her frail arms wind-milling in wrinkled little loops.

I jumped from my car. "Sorry lady!" I called out and limped to the front of the car to check out my bumper. Just as I feared there was a long jagged scratch on it. There was no way that was going to buff out. Damn.

"Hey!" The old woman shouted. "Come over here and hold me up. You almost killed me you crazy bastard."

I made my way over to her. "I'm really sorry lady, are you okay?"

"Where'd you get your driver's license, at the zoo?"

"I said I was sorry."

"You're not nearly as sorry as you're going to be. I'm calling my lawyer when I get home."

"Ma'am, will you please just calm down? What can I do for you?"

"You can help me to my car and then find my walker." She peered at me over her glasses. "God you even look like a lunatic. What happened to your face?"

"It's ...it's a long story. You drove here?"

"Yes, I drove numbskull. My helicopter is in the shop. You think I can't drive just because I'm old? I can drive better than you apparently."

I got her to her car and then left to retrieve her walker. It was smashed to bits. Damn again. All this walking was killing my ankle too.

"Your walker's a goner," I said as I lurched up to her car. "Here let me pay for it. How much was it, fifty dollars?"

"You cheap shit, that was a Volaris. It cost my insurance company over three hundred dollars."

"Dear God!"

"Why are you shuffling around like a damn zombie? Are you retarded or something?"

"I've had a bad week."

"Well it's going to get worse."

"I do wish you would quit threatening me."

"I don't know how I'm going to get in the house when I get home without my walker. You are going to pay for a new one you know."

"Can't you call somebody to help?"

"Like a family member?" She leaned out the window and spat a big lugy on my shoe. "My lazy ass son sits around all day and smokes medicinal marijuana. A fifty-eight-year-old pot head. And my pathetic daughter went to California years ago to make movies. I think she ended up in the porn industry."

"Good God!"

"You might have seen her in a couple of films."

"I don't..."

"What can we do, right? You have any kids?"

"No I don't."

"That's probably for the best. You'd have probably backed over them with your car by now."

I looked at my watch. I had a lawnmower to buy. "Maybe I can follow you home and help you in the house."

"Oh you'd like that wouldn't you? You could come over and peep in the windows."

"There's no way in hell I'd do that."

"Don't get all red in the face, it makes you look scary. I was just bustin' your balls."

So I followed the old bat home and got her in the house.

The whole time we were inching up her broken sidewalk I kept one eye on my surroundings. It wasn't the best of neighborhoods.

A deep, thick barking sound came from behind a door down the hallway. "What is that?" I asked.

"It's just Jasper. He smells a stranger."

"Look I hate to ask you this but I have to go pee."

"It's down the hallway, first door on the right."

"Is it safe?"

"Yeah, just don't open the door on the left."

"First door on the left," I thought as I made my way, zombie-like, down the hallway. I flung open the door looking for relief but found a portal to Hell. A great black dog leaped at my throat. As I staggered backwards I tripped over a rug and fell, probably saving my life. The Rottweiler ripped a hole in my pants and a second hole in my ass, there was blood.

"Stop it Jasper!" the old lady yelled. She picked up a *People Magazine* and started whacking Jasper with it. Miley Cyrus's face was bouncing off a Rottweiler's ass, which seemed inspired somehow. Finally Jasper got bored.

"I'll send you the money for the walker." I called out as I made for the door. Outside I leaned on the porch railing and stared at my car. It was up on blocks. All four wheels were gone. I called Denise.

"Did you buy a lawnmower?" She asked.

"No, I'm waiting for AAA."

"What happened?"

"We need to buy new wheels and tires for the car. We have to buy a three hundred dollar walker too by the way."

"What?"

"My pants are torn, I pissed in them, and I'm bleeding. I don't think I'm going to be buying a mower today. I'll get back to you." I hung up and as I sat on the old lady's front porch staring at the setting sun, I heard someone nearby singing in Spanish. A little further away I heard the unmistakable sound of gunfire.

After much pleading, Relax Cab Service finally sent a car

over that never did come to a full stop when he picked me up. I had to jump in, banging my ankle and almost screaming out my address. Amazingly the driver was American, but surly in manner and played his music so loud I could feel the bass thumping. It was jazz fusion I think. I never did get to relax.

(September 6th)

My wife keeps reminding me that the yard hasn't been mowed yet and tomorrow is the day we're having friends over. I got back on the phone.

I called up a "friend" whose dog I've been sitting three weeks out of every four for the last six months. He brings the dog over, drops her off and flies away to Africa to shoot Cape Buffalo, or South America to float down the Amazon, to California to fight wildfires, or who-the-hell-knows where else. Sometimes I have to call him, collect, "Hey man, you do remember you have a dog?"

"Oh yeah," He says. "Yeah, yeah." Then he'll keep her a week before she suddenly reappears and he's gone again. As a matter of fact she's here right now, licking my good ankle. What pisses me off, of course, is while he's roping steer in Montana I'm double-scooping poop. He wrestled alligators in the Florida Everglades last month. The last thing I wrestled was a Briggs and Stratton, which kicked my ass. He answered the phone.

"Pierre?" I said.

"Oh hello." He answered cautiously. "Whom might this be?"

Whom. "This is the man whom apparently has full custody of your dog but you're more than welcome to exercise your visitation rights whenever you please."

"Ahh...I'm sorry Dan. I just got back in town and was on my way to pick her up just this moment. How's my little Francis doing?"

"A lot better than I am. Look I need you to do something for me for a change."

"Anything, my friend. Just name it."

"I need you to mow my yard."

"You're joking."

"I'm not in a joking mood there, Pierre."

"You sound a little on edge there Dan. Is all okay?"

"It could be the medication. What about the yard?"

"Well, you see Dan, I don't really mow yards per se. I have a service."

"Can you arrange for your service to mow my yard and pay for it? I mean I have been keeping your dog for the better part of six months now. I bet she doesn't even remember you."

"My word, I thought we did favors for each other, my good man, you know, gratis."

I realized something at that particular moment, I hated Pierre's guts. All these phony mannerisms and speech patterns he can't get right. I don't even think his real name is Pierre. It's Elmo or something like that.

"Here's the deal la Pierre. Either you send your service over to mow my yard or I'm slitting little Francis's throat and feeding her to the crows."

"You wouldn't dare!"

"Actually I would dare. It would be doing both of us a favor, Francis too. That is one confused little puppy."

Two hours later I was enjoying the smell of freshly cut grass. I heard my wife talking on the phone in an unusually furtive voice. "We need to talk," she said after she hung up, and we did.

(September 7th)

Well it's certainly been an interesting four days. I destroyed my lawn mower, caught my face on fire, guaranteed my neighbor will never speak to me again, got bit by a dog, almost killed an old lady, had my car stripped, and screwed up my ankle. Oh yeah, I almost forgot, my wife ran off with another man. Well I don't really consider him a man, it was Pierre. I don't know what that says about me.

69

On the positive side, x-rays revealed my ankle is badly sprained but not broken, the bite wounds were superficial and the dog proved not to be rabid, insurance took care of the car, the old woman decided not to sue, and I saw some very well done nude photographs of my newly alienated neighbor's wife. My wife? God that woman was needy. So everything is pretty much a wash.

"We need to talk." She said. I thought we were going to discuss burgers and franks. She was just going to be frank.

"I'm leaving," she said without having to clear her throat. "You're immature, irresponsible, incompetent, and ignorant."

"That's a lot of words that start with "i", I said. "Where are you going?"

"I don't know...everywhere. Pierre said he would show me the world. Your idea of a good time is going to Hooters."

"I like Hooters."

"Exactly.

"But I was going to surprise you with a trip to Jamaica."

"Right, Jamaica. Don't you think one surprise a day is enough for one marriage? I do not want to go anywhere with you. I would tell you to take care of yourself but I'm sure I'll be reading about you in the papers any day now."

"My goodness," I thought. "I'm living a country music song."

I looked at myself in the mirror and considered my dating prospects to be pretty slim. Not that I'd have much time for dating because of the extra job I'll need to work to pay for lawn mowers, walkers, doctor bills, and divorce proceedings, Yep, I've got a pretty shitty life ahead of me. But at least next week, I'm on vacation.

.

Myth Amerca

Do you know that half of everything you know is probably wrong? It's not because you're a dumbass. You've just been misinformed, misled, or flat out lied to. I'm talking about important stuff here. Not the lies the President told. If you believed those, well ... you actually are a dumbass.

For instance, I bet you thought poinsettia leaves were poisonous. They are not! You'd have to eat about 60 leaves to even get a belly ache. I wish I had known about this a before I wasted a lot of money and effort trying to poison my wife. A few years ago around Christmas time, my wife really pissed me off about something. I can't remember now what it was, but at the time seemed important enough to do her in with poinsettia leaves. I slipped some in her food a little at a time. This had some delicious irony to it because I'd suspected for years she was trying to kill me with her cooking.

There was absolutely no visible effect. I figured it was a slow-acting poison and would do its job eventually. I was counting on time to work its magic. Thankfully it didn't because I'm not mad anymore and also her cooking has improved dramatically.

I've always heard that you shouldn't go for a swim for at least an hour after lunch. Since I can't swim at all I thought this was great advice for breakfast and dinner as well. But apparently food in the belly doesn't immobilize your arms and legs. Physiologically this makes sense, but after I eat somehow the only part of my body that works is my right thumb placed strategically on the TV remote. This phenomenon can last at least an hour or more, or until my wife finishes the dishes. So this belief is only wrong for other people.

Here's another one; eating snow will make you sick. It will, if there's a little spiral dog turd on top of the snow cone you're chowing down on. A study published back when the Earth was flat said that snowflakes may form around a "seed" of bacteria

71

called Pseudomonas syringae. I hate writing words like that because, unless you're a scientist or a hypochondriac, you'll just skim right past them. Most people don't like to read words that are hard to pronounce and they can't use at parties later.

"Hey man, did you know that snowflakes have Petaluma syringes in them?"

"Shut up jackass, you're drunk."

As it turns out that particular bacteria only kills beans and tomatoes. That's why it's a really bad idea to plant a garden in late December. So unless you are a bean or a tomato it's okay to eat snow, but in moderation of course. Consuming too much snow will make you sterile. Nah, just kidding. But you may get snowballs.

Another line of bullshit we've been fed is to drink eight 8-ounce glasses of water a day. I'm so sick of this one I want to puke, clear liquids, through my nose. How could a person possibly benefit from swigging down this much H2O? I've done a lot of my own personal research to disprove this myth. For example, beer is mostly water and sometimes after I drink from 10 to 12 12-ounce glasses a day I feel like shit. I have to be honest with you. I wake up all cranky and the first thing I think is "Damn I drank too much last night." Not "I should have drunk more."

I tried sucking down that much water once and got fired from a really good job. I couldn't stay out of the bathroom. I tried explaining to my boss that it was for my health but he just said "You don't need to be healthy just be on your job." What a tyrant. You'd think an air-traffic controller supervisor would be more understanding. Planes nowadays practically land themselves you know.

"If you cross your eyes they'll get stuck like that." This is something our mothers told us so she wouldn't have to explain to strangers that her children weren't nincompoops.

I once dated a cross-eyed girl. She was bright, witty, and had a set of tits that still brings a tear to my eye when I think of how close I was to laying claim to them. After I became comfortable enough in our relationship I asked her one day if she had crossed her eyes on purpose and they had gotten stuck that way. She promptly lifted her blouse and said, "Take a look at these, smartass because it's the only time you're ever going to see them." This temporarily crossed MY eyes but by the time I got home, alone, they were back to normal; the tears, they still come.

Sugar makes you hyper. Kids hear this all the time. No, sugar will rot your teeth and make you fat, but it doesn't make kids bounce off the walls. The hyper comes from the adrenaline rush of being around a bunch of their playmates at birthday parties where there are grandparents and clowns, not to be redundant, to protect their scheming little asses.

As I grew older and the birthday cake was replaced with a keg as the centerpiece at birthday parties, I missed that adrenaline rush. People who do keg stands tend not to be quite as energetic while busy puking in the bushes. I turned to crystal meth to get that rush and, well, became an outcast, a loner, a thief and a beggar. I alienated my friends and family and started writing poetry like this:

Grateful I became
Less so
The wanderer of wonders
Thoughts that came rushing
From where they fled
Who's Earnest?

I miss you sugar. Please come back.

Has anyone ever told you "Don't wake up someone who's walking in their sleep?" Well if they have you should ask them "...and why not?" Here you are trying to sleep off a hangover and some idiot that was too wasted to drive home is up doing the zombie-walk, bumping into shit, and turning over the fish bowl. This is a fantastic time to screw with them a little bit. I keep a flashing blue light at my house for just this purpose. I turn it on, grab and shake them, duck, and then yell, "Sir, have you been drinking?!" Trust me it's funny as shit.

Two quick myths. Cracking your knuckles will give you

arthritis. This is untrue. It may annoy someone so much that they crack their knuckles over your head causing pain unrelated to arthritis.

You can see the Great Wall of China from outer space. No you cannot. I've travelled extensively in outer space, mostly on business, and I've never seen anything remotely resembling the Great Wall. If you don't believe me (and why would you?) one of China's own astronauts, Yur Yan King Mi, disproved the myth. He said, and I'm paraphrasing here, "Somebody must have moved the wall because I don't see it." Moving the wall would be a good prank but who has time for that?

My favorite myths have to do with something everyone does but no one talks about. You may have done it as recently as this morning. You may be doing it right now as you read this. If you are I really don't want to know about it. I'm not talking about farting. I'm talking about masturbation. Apparently from ninety-five to ninety-eight percent of people do it. So when you feel like you're surrounded by a bunch of jerk-offs, you're right! Anyway, one myth is that girls don't masturbate. But they do! Isn't that great? Now I don't know, nor want to know, what girls think about when they masturbate but the thought of them masturbating makes me want to.

Another myth is that it cause blindness and make hair grow on the palm of your hand. I wear glasses. I have hair on the back of my hands. Maybe this is not a myth. Maybe it means that although I've been doing it for a while, like everything else I do concerning sex, I'm doing it wrong. Maybe I'm being punished for my deviant behavior. I feel so guilty. I'm kidding of course. If loving myself is wrong I don't want to be right.

This brings us to the biggest myth of all. "Men think about sex every seven seconds". That's a barefaced lie. We never stop thinking about it. Even the one or two professors who understand quantum physics. "Now students, the Planck-Einstein equation and de Broglie wavelength relations...dear God I'd like to have a relation with that blonde in the third row. Uh, did I say that out loud?" Every seven seconds? No man is strong enough to go that long. Besides what else could we possibly have to think about?

Where do all these myths come from? Did someone lose their sight from pleasuring themselves? Did someone eat snow and die? Did someone drink eight glasses of water in one day and suddenly become faster than a speeding bullet? I think someone with too much time on their hands decided to make up a lie and see how many people would fall for it, how far they could go with it. Why, I bet if you had a good enough lie, you could take it all the way to the White House.

Til Death Do Us...

I love my wife, I just wouldn't want to do extended jail time with her. I'm a hopeless romantic that way.

Throughout history, married couples have committed all sorts of dastardly crimes, from espionage to serial killings, perhaps in an attempt to spice up their marriage. I've heard sometimes they can grow stale. I wouldn't know.

But none of these adventurous couples, if they escaped "Old Sparky", did time in the same cell together. They paid their debt to society at different locations, far, far away. This is not a very effective deterrent to crime.

None of them believed they were going to get caught, of course. We, I mean they, never do. If they had considered for a moment there was a possibility of spending the rest of their lives together, looking at each other, listening to those same whiny complaints, over and over, the days drawing out to hours, the hours to minutes, until every second pounded like a death knell in their head. Until the dreams they share are their hands closing around the throat of the person sleeping in the bunk below them, or above. "Oh my God," they realize. "We're in this thing for life!" If a spark of sanity had branded their consciousness for a moment, at least one of them would surely have said, "Hey let's stop and think about what we're getting ready to do for a minute. We may live to regret this more than we could possibly imagine."

Oh there's a chance, if they were deeply, madly, in love their passion inflamed by the bludgeoning and disemboweling they shared, that they wouldn't sell each other down the river at the trial to save their own sorry asses. It's feasible they would cross the threshold of their cement love nest still starry-eyed for one another. But if love is a dream, the big house is an alarm clock. Yes sir, love on The Rock.

You know what the male of the newly incarcerated couple is thinking. "We've got plenty of time on our hands with nothing to do so we might as well do each other."

Now I can't speak for every married man out there, actually I can only speak for this one off the record, but I can't help but think of that joke, "Have you heard of the new Playboy magazine for married men? The same centerfold every month." And that's the least of their problems.

Besides unprovoked violence, unimaginative food, and acute boredom there's the ever-present danger of nagging. "Did you lock the door?" The wife asks before they turn in for the night.

"It's always locked." The husband answers.

"What are you making there?" She peers over his shoulder, so close he can feel her breath on his neck, again.

"It's called a shank, keep your voice down."

"It looks dangerous. Who are you planning to stab with that?"

"Oh, I've got an idea."

"What's that on your arm? Another tattoo?"

"It's just a number to let everybody know I've got friends in here."

"I wish you wouldn't hang out with those people, they're hoodlums."

"Yuh think?"

"I just have such a hard time making new friends." The wife sniffles.

The husband puts a keener edge on his shank.

Being married for many years has its rewards. Knowing someone is always there for you, to support you no matter what; the love and the laughter. On the flip side you certainly know how to turn those screws and push those buttons to drive each other crazy. It's kinda special.

That's why I don't go out and commit mayhem with my wife no matter how much she begs. I don't know where she gets this violent streak from. She used to be so sweet and gentle. We have been together for quite some time now but I don't see what that has to do with anything. I do have wild mood swings, from deep, dark lows to manic highs. Sometimes the voices in my head let loose with a wail and a keen making me shout to drown them out. I drink heavily and puke in inconvenient places. I do have the tendency to fly off the handle at the least provocation, staying mad for months. These are the things that make me more interesting. How can twenty two years of blissful marriage make a woman change that much?

Anyway, I'm not getting caught up in her little Bonnie and Clyde fantasies. What if they suddenly changed the sentencing to "You do the crime together, you do the time together"? I'm afraid if my wife and I were thrown into the pokey simultaneously it would spoil what we have.

One thing for certain though, we'd have the tidiest cell on the block, and we'd drive each other mad because of it. I couldn't hide things between the sofa cushions anymore or cram them into my desk drawers.

"Hang up your orange jumpsuit. Do you think I want to spend the rest of my life sentence picking up after you?"

"You should have thought about that before you pulled out that gun." I mutter to myself.

"What?"

"Nothing."

My idea of helping my wife with housework has always been to make myself as scarce as possible. Just get out of the way of flying dust mops and trampling vacuum cleaners.

Her latest big complaint is the amount of hair I'm leaving on my bathroom floor. There's a couple of things I want to say to her like, "Well darling, love of my life, don't you think I'd much rather keep my hair on my head instead of it falling out and cascading down like the leaves of autumn?" or "You know, sweetheart, I thought that was why we had separate bathrooms. Yours could remain clean enough to entertain guests if you wished and mine could look like where elephants go to die."

I thought these were fine answers at first but quickly realized she wanted something more concrete. "Honey," I said. "Honestly, I'm leaving the hair down because human hair repels wild animals. You haven't seen any deer, rabbits, or squirrels feeding on my plants in there have you?"

"Danny, you don't have any plants in there. They couldn't survive the noxious fumes. No life form that can be seen with the naked eye could survive in there."

I thought this a bit harsh but did promise to try to do better. That's all I can do really, is promise, because I know I'll never be able to measure up to her standard of neat. The lead snapped off my pencil one day, rolled across the floor, and under a chair. I looked for it for hours to no avail but my wife found it by accident while cleaning the crevasses between the boards of the floor with a toothbrush.

"Look." She held out her hand and in her palm laid the offending piece of lead. I was wearing my glasses at the moment so I barely had to squint. "I'm not trying to be mean," she said in that voice that lets me know how patient she is being. "But can you please pick up after yourself?" And prison guards think they will come in, unannounced, and toss our cell? I scoff.

I write the warden begging for thirty to sixty days in solitary confinement. "She won't stop making the beds, sir, or hounding me to clean the toilet. I just need some rest."

Maybe we'd receive a pardon because we'd both "suffered enough" and go home to build a new life together. We could start a support group scam under the guise of warning others of the dangers of cohabitation incarceration. "You have no idea the hell we've been through." We sell CDs, books, and DVDs. We get rich on the speaking circuit. Then the ACLU sticks its nose in and protests that husband and wife being forced to do time together is cruel and unusual punishment. As much as I enjoy ridiculing everything they stand for, this is one time I have to agree.

So the next time I ask my wife what we're doing tonight and she says "Why don't we go knock over a convenience store," I'll laugh and pat her pretty little head.

"No, let's stop and think about this little darling, it might be something we regret for the rest of our lives."

Mexican Insurance

I was in the big town of Liberty last night. I go down there sometimes to pick up blood, urine, and other things I learned not to talk about on a first date, from a specimen lock-box. No, it's not a hobby, it's my job.

Although the parking lot was well lit it was also very much deserted. As I loaded my haul into the car I was approached by three gentlemen some would call "undocumented aliens." They looked like Mexicans to me.

Seeing the word "lab" on the side of my car they mistakenly thought I was carrying drugs and demanded I hand over the contents of my bag.

"Whoa ho ho there mi amigos," I said. "You don't want what's in this bag." But they thought they did, and sometimes that's good enough.

While two of them held me the third grabbed the bag out of my hand and started rifling through the contents. Finding nothing they wanted to smoke, snort, inject, or most definitely swallow, they demanded money.

"Me das tu dinero, pendejo!" One of them spit out at me.

Now I don't speak that Mexican but I knew he wasn't asking me if I wanted some dinero. "You're going to be just as disappointed there too, mi comprades." I replied. And they were. I think I had like a dollar and twenty-three cents on me.

To mask the humiliation they must have felt for having to resort to a life of drugs and violence here in the land of plenty, the good old US of A, they took to whacking on me like a piñata, pounding on me about the head and shoulders with occasional forays into the torso area.

As I fell to the ground I noticed the light was on at the Nationwide Insurance office next door to the medical clinic where I just picked up. The agent, bless his little over-stressed heart, was still sitting at this desk working diligently.

One of the undocumented aliens, who still looked like a

Mexican to me, lost his balance and fell when he tried to kick me in the head with his little pointy-toed cowboy boot. I saw my opening.

Scrambling to my feet, I lunged toward the insurance office door and was halfway in when the Mexican posse caught me from behind.

"Mister!" I yelled. "Are you on my side?" I had heard somewhere that he was.

Quickly sizing up the situation, he figured none of my attackers were clients of his. Anyone involved in an accident with an undocumented alien knows they're never insured, and erring on the side of caution to prevent me from filing an accidental death and dismemberment claim in case I was a client, he jumped up from his desk and said, "You damn right I am." I was relieved.

Ripping off his coat and tie and rolling up his sleeves, he tore through the door and waded in amongst them. Holy Alamo, this man was a go-getter. I tried to help, I surely did, but after a few moments I realized I was just in the way. I stepped back and watched a professional go to work. He threw haymakers with full coverage, whipped out a double indemnity, and brought down the deductible without breaking a sweat. His Van Heusen was covered in blood and none of it was his. The last I saw of the Mexicans they were making a run for the border.

My new friend? He wasn't even breathing hard. I thanked him and he handed me his card. "When you get a chance, drop by and we'll take a look at your life insurance policy." He said. "You know, you can never have enough."

Safely back in my car, travelling down the highway, listening to smooth contemporary jazz, and drinking one of those big soft drinks that was almost illegal in New York, I realized the agent had given me some good, sound advice. That was a pretty close call back there. I was also very pleased that had been a Nationwide Insurance office instead of one of their competitors. I don't think old Flo could have provided that same level of service, or that little lizard either.

Shooting Star

You ever read something, read something in a newspaper or a magazine that makes you go, "What in the hell?" Like the other day I read in Time Magazine that the United States of America is the world's largest exporter of sperm. That's right sperm. Could this be America's next great untapped natural resource?

Now somebody at Time Magazine thought this was important enough information that they needed to share it with the world. They must have been right because it certainly got my attention. All these years I had no idea I needed this information.

But I didn't know we exported anything anymore because I didn't know we made anything anymore. I guess we're producing something more important than sofas and socks. We're helping populate the planet with even more funny looking kids.

"Now wait a damn minute!" you might be saying right now, and I feel ya. You want to know where all this cum is flying off to. "Do I need to duck while I'm on vacation, say, down in Anguilla? Does my lady need to keep her legs closed in St. Tropez?" Relax. It looks like all that strong American jizz is making its way to willing vaginas mostly in Canada and Australia. Although some of it is trickling down legs in the Philippines, Vietnam, and Mexico. The Caribbean seems to be fairly safe right now. Still. If we're going to populate the seven extra states Obama thinks we have, we'd better get busy down there too.

I must admit that artificial insemination is the only thing I know less about than international politics, but I can still surmise as good as the next fool. I'm thinking we've always been on good terms with Canada and Australia, never invaded their country as peacekeepers, fired a shot at them in anger, and now I know why; armed conflict with these two nations would be like civil war. "You can't shoot him, he might be your brother." But according to the hot shot of bodily fluids at *Time*, we ain't shooting blanks no more.

Another thing, when I think of Canada and Australia, I think, white people. And since shooting your wad in a jar for fun and profit sounds like something white people would do, it would be only natural that these two countries would be our best customers.

The Philippines? I don't know, beats the shit out of me. I've met enough Filipinos to know they're all crazy and want to be just like us, you know, American, with their own reality show. To be fair I've only met one Filipino, but trust me, this bitch was crazy, so until I meet another one a hundred percent is a hundred percent in anyone's book. If I meet another Filipino, and she doesn't try to castrate me with a butcher knife for sleeping with her best friend, I'll possibly do a re-evaluation. While I'm at it I'll ask about their craving for Uncle Sam's nut butter.

Now although we withdrew our troops from Vietnam decades ago some of the troops didn't pull out in time. They left behind many round-eyed American byproducts that would love to have a child that looks like them, hence the Vietnamese market.

Mexico? No se, es mejor que mierda vete mi. Now don't get me wrong. I'm truly grateful to all those hombres that swam the Rio Grande and started giving our poor, lonely fat girls some loving. Not that I give a rat's ass about their chubby little love life, but if they're home riding Julio like a little brown pony then the buffet line at Golden Corral will move along at a much faster clip. But why are we shooting our cum south of the border? When you look at the condition their country's in you'd think more babies is last thing they'd need.

Once more, now this is just a theory, but maybe, just maybe those chiquitas are thinking if they have a baby from an American donor the Democrats will mail them a citizenship right before the next election. It ain't that farfetched.

You have to give it to those hot-blooded Latinos, they are

industrious. But how many more dishwashers, construction workers, and gardeners do we need sending their money back to La Cucaracha? Wake up America, they're invading our country from within. I know this sounds like something from an idiotic James Patterson novel but paranoia is real popular right now and I wanted to get in on some of that action myself. The Chinese are trying to poison our children with lead too, by the way.

The Time Magazine article stated that a man could get paid as much as $500 per ejaculation, something most guys gladly do for free, and can earn $30,000 a year if he can produce good thick jizz with strong-swimming sperm. I swear I'm not making this up. When I thought of all the potential earnings I threw around with reckless abandon in my youth it made me want to weep. There I was, young, dumb, and full of...money.

But reading further I saw where you had to have a Ph.D. to get that kind of dough. To get a lousy $60 you have to have at least a college degree. I didn't realize you had to be educated to do this type of work. It's mostly just working with your hands anyway. I know complete idiots who have children. I bet you do too.

Unfortunately they not only profile you by education but by appearance too. So that's that. With my credentials my sperm would fetch about the same price as gasoline; three dollars and twenty-three cents a gallon currently. I'd be all tuckered out and still bouncing checks. I'd be better off picking up tin cans from the side of the road. At least I'd have something left when I got home at night.

Some childless couples, single women, and...lesbians are seeking sperm donors over the Internet, making it much more convenient to shop. A woman can pick her baby's daddy easier than choosing which pair of shoes she wants this week. Except for lesbians, who only wear comfortable shoes. The mama wannabe can send a picture of her non-virile husband, or if he's repugnant, Brad Pitt, and the facial-recognition software finds a donor that closest resembles her request. Nine months later, ta-da, she has something Angelina Jolie had to wait years for, a

Caucasian baby. "Look," the new mom exclaims to a friend. "My baby Derek looks just like a little Brad Pitt."

Her friend, who sprang for the much cheaper supply of my sperm replies, "Well, my baby Elmer looks like a little peach pit but I got such a good deal on him I was able to buy these new shoes, ain't they cute." You have to give it to some women, they do know how to shop.

A few people that have a conscience, and I know some that actually do, may be disturbed by the moral and social implications created by single women, and...lesbians, who choose to eliminate the father figure from their mail-order baby's life. Granted this does prevent a lot of men from being fathers on the lam but shouldn't junior at least have to chance to grow up knowing his dad is a deadbeat?

As crazy as the Muslims are, and they are some crazy sons-of-bitches, they do have the common sense to ban single mothers and...lesbians, from access to sperm. I bet when lesbians made this lifestyle choice they never dreamed this would be a problem. Anyway, even married women in Muslim countries must get their husband's approval. This makes sense too.

Let's say Ali Baba Oxenfree is watching Fox News, getting more and more pissed off, merely contemplating strapping on a bomb at this point, when his wife walks in announcing she's pregnant by a man she's never met, thus pushing Ali over the edge into martyrdom. If seeing a woman's hair is enough to set these fools off, what's a batch of infidel jizz going to do? Ali wants to know that those little future terrorists, playing like they're hijacking a plane out in the yard, are his.

Being part of a child's life never entered the equation for most donors, like that numbskull up in Virginia who can claim over 70 offspring around the world and maybe as many as over 140. Can you imagine the number of t-ball games he'd have to attend? I guess since he's college-educated he could figure out a way to consolidate and have a whole league of his own little tax write-offs. But this is never going to be a problem because he said, "I don't see them as my kids." And he was chosen as a donor because he's intelligent?

But 140 is nothing compared to a man in Great Britain who has sired over 1,000 kids in a thirty-year span. Here the world is full of bastards and those morons are out there making more.

Responsibility, they should just take that word out of the dictionary because no one knows its meaning anymore. With all these little half-brothers and sisters running around that don't know each other did anyone consider they may meet, and mate, creating a second West Virginia. Who in the hell needs that?

What id one of those brainy PhDs strike it rich and a little stranger shows up at their door one day with their hand out? "Just show me the money Daddy."

What if someone gets stuck with a defective child? One that just stares at a tiny hand-held screen all day, tapping out words in a cryptic code. You just can't return them, minus shipping and handling. Just because a guy has sex with a jar doesn't mean it's not personal on some level.

Now the world's largest sperm bank is in ... wait for it . . California. I bet you didn't see that coming. Right now there's an intellectual out in Berkeley, with a degree in Medieval Literature, using all that education to shovel French fries into a sack down at the old In-N-Out burger. He *was* thinking, "My life sucks. I'm going to kill myself." Then he read the *Time Magazine* article and it changed his life. "Hey, I'm an educated man. I'm going down to the world's largest sperm bank and make a deposit, start making some real money!" Not so fast there my little learned liberal, don't get yourself excited just yet. One of your fellow Californians has been hard at work fathering fifteen children already by *giving* away fresh sperm, for free.

And that, that's why the economy sucks.

Will There Be Cake?

There's a retired deputy-sheriff that lives in my neighborhood. He's a nice enough fella. He doesn't chase bad guys anymore, though he still runs to keep his weight down. It seems to be working; he's not getting any fatter. He patrols our streets occasionally, just looking around, our own one-man neighborhood-watch like those that seem to be so popular down Sanford, Florida way. Talking to him can be a bit unnerving as he tends to interrogate instead of talk which puts you on the defensive even if he's just asking what kind of dog you have.

"He's a shi-tzu, which translates to "lion dog" in Mandarin you know. He's descended from the Chinese wolf. He's a great guard dog even though he's kinda little. He barks a lot and loud too, so it would give me plenty of time to get out of bed and get my legally registered firearm in case of a break-in or home invasion." At this point I realize I'm raving like a lunatic and clamp my jaw shut.

"Where'd you get him?"

"We got him off death row at the pound."

"Do you keep him on a leash? Does he bite?"

"Uh...yes, always. Even in the house. He bit my mother-in-law once so I think that makes him a good dog to have around." My attempt at humor went unappreciated.

"Yeah, well, he's a cute little dog." The deputy, retired, says and moves on.

Four or five years ago I received a jury summons and since this was my fifth call to serve I felt I'd done all the civic duty I needed to do. I'm not really the citizen type. I called upon my deputy friend, who was still active at the time, to help me out if he could. I figured he had some good connections down at the local law house. He could "call in a few favors" if that's the way they talk when they're not on TV.

"Well you know you get paid to serve, don't you?"

87

I did know this, a whopping twenty dollars a day if I remembered correctly. Though that's great money to a ten-year-old making sneakers in Singapore I need more than a straw mat to lie down on. "Can you help me out this one time, Deputy Dave?" I said. He did. He came through for me.

Six months later I received another jury summons in the mail. This letter had a slightly different tone than the previous one. The legalese, loosely translated, stated I should get my white ass down to the courthouse right away and don't be late. "What is this?" I said to myself as I walked up the driveway scratching my head. Apparently the good constable hadn't come through for me after all. He had merely delayed the process. Meanwhile, I had inadvertently pissed somebody off.

So off I go down to the courthouse with all kinds of advice looping through my noggin. "You want to get out of jury duty?" My well-meaning friends asked. "Tell them you're hard of hearing. Tell them you have bladder control issues and can't sit still for long periods of time. Tell them all black people are guilty, you can tell just by looking at them (My black friends suggested that one). Tell them your uncle died in Alaska and you're the only one in the family that speaks Inuit."

I discovered something about my friends from all this advice. No matter their ethnicity, education, religion, creed, or color, they're idiots. I love 'em but they're idiots.

I show up for jury duty with my big plan and lo and behold there is no interview, there are no questions from a snarky lawyer. No sir, my name is called and I sit in a jury box with seventeen other yahoos who were picked for Grand Jury. We don't serve for a week or so. That's why we are called the Grand Jury, we serve for a WHOLE YEAR! Thank you very much, Deputy Dave.

So I was out walking my maniacal dog one afternoon after serving my time when I was approached by the Deputy.

"Howdy neighbor," he said. "How are you doing?"

"Fine," I answered cautiously because I had a whole new respect for him. Previously I had thought him merely an over-zealous protector of the cul-de-sac. I had under-estimated him.

He had the power to screw me royally. "Sir." I finished.

"That's great. Look, I need you to do me a favor."

I couldn't think of what this man could possibly need from me. I looked at my dog. He seemed perplexed also.

"As you know this is an election year." He went on.

"It sure is and I think it's every Americans duty to get out and vote." I had hoped that covered the favor he needed. As he droned on I noticed an army of ants near my feet dragging what looked like the remains of a sparrow. I was thinking how ants are fun to watch and how I wished I had gotten an ant farm when I was small and how I could buy one now since I'm basically an adult with my own money and... "What?"

"I said I need you to come by my house about three o'clock this afternoon if you can. You know we have a convicted felon running for sheriff and I certainly don't want to work for him again."

"Ah, Sheriff Haggis, he certainly was popular while he was in office. Of course, I never got arrested by him."

"You never had to work for him either. Sheriff Grace is a fine man and we need to support him in every way. I'm trying to get as many people from the neighborhood as possible to drop by. It would make me look good to the boss." He laughed but his eyes never left mine. What he meant was "don't make me look bad." I had already had one year to think about it.

So three o'clock rolled around and, as August in North Carolina tends to be, it was hotter'n hell out on Deputy Dave's patio. I was sweating like *I* was the one running for re-election. I tried to make small talk with a bunch of people either I didn't know, didn't like, or downright loathed. You damn right I was having a good time.

We were washing down peanuts and pretzels with tropical punch served in those little paper cups the size of shot glasses. I had sucked down about seven or eight of those little teaser cups and was still thirsty. I could have stuck my whole head in the punch bowl. I probably would have if it had been a Christmas party. The centerpiece of this little soiree was a sheet cake inscribed with "Keep Sheriff Grace". It's been my experience that sheet cakes taste like puffy sugar spread across dry bread. Yummy.

"Have you tried the cake?" Deputy Dave asked.

"I'm good." I said.

"I think you should try the cake."

It didn't sound like an invitation so I tried the cake. Everyone else had carefully cut around the "Keep Sheriff Grace" but with dexterity I didn't know I possessed, I managed to cut out all the letters except "p-i-g", it was a *big* piece of cake.

"I want you to meet my boss." Deputy Dave said, guiding me over to where a beefy man eating a fistful of peanuts stood.

For the life of me I can't remember his name or his title, maybe Assistant Sheriff or Vice-Sheriff, something. What I do remember is he had the worst set of teeth I've ever seen on someone who is employed. He whistled through them when he spoke. I think he realized this and sometimes stumbled over some other words as well.

"Nisss to meet ya." He said. "Thisss isss a good party. You lifh in thisss nabuhood?"

The good deputy then took me to meet the sheriff. "This is my real boss." He said.

"Ah, Sheriff Grace. Nice to meet you." He was a round-face man with a winning smile. My kind of people, a politician with a gun.

"I like what you did with the cake. I like a sense of humor. I hope I can count on your vote."

Deputy Dave looked at the cake and frowned at me. "Yes sir," I said to Sheriff Grace. "You can count on me. I wish I had two votes to give you."

The sheriff smiled politely. The deputy still frowned.

"Wow is it 3:15 already?" I looked at my watch. "Well it was nice to meet you but I really need to get going." Once more I felt I had done my civic duty as a conscientious citizen.

Later on that hot August I was driving down one of our county's scenic roads, still pissed off about those fifteen minutes I gave Deputy Dave. Fifteen hot, sweaty, nasty, boring minutes that left a bad taste in my mouth. Very much like sex with my ex-wife. Anyway, the way I saw it he still owed me a favor, one that I'd never get from him. Dammit, I wanted my favor. I hate it when people owe me. I'd rather owe them, that way I wield the power. They'll always want something from me. That's the kind of thinking you can acquire when you don't have a conscience.

For the umpteenth time I passed a "Grace for Sheriff" sign but this time I said out loud, "Aw, screw Sheriff Grace, right in the ass." That got me thinking about Pulp Fiction of course. This time though it was Sheriff Grace bent over with the ball gag in his mouth. One of our county's finest meth dealers is having his way with him while another stands nearby with a gun trained on the Vice-Sheriff.

"Ungh. Umgh." The sheriff grunts, his eyes bulge, thinning hair awry, he sweats profusely.

After a minute or two the first meth dealer says, "Come on over here bad teeth and get you some of this."

"Nuh-uh. I ain't running for nuffin."

"Well you didn't exactly run from it last night now did you?"

"Huh?" Sheriff Grace looks at his deputy, lank hair falls into his left eye. He's having one of his worst days in office.

"Oh you dirty dog, dirty dog." Bad teeth says.

I laughed and laughed at that image. I think it represented common man's feeling of hopelessness and loss of faith in a system that increasingly excludes him and renders his voice obsolete. Or I could be a perv. Either one works for me.

Regardless, I thought it was so funny that I accidently pushed down on the gas pedal. Pretty soon I was flying down the highway. Too late I saw the blue light behind me.

"Goodness," I said. "Is that old Bad Teeth?"

"Howdy," He said. "I thought that wasss you. You know you were going a little fassst back there."

"Yeah, sorry about that but to be honest I got to take a dump real bad and I was hurrying home."

"Sssorry to hear that."

"That's okay, it happens almost every day."

"Well lisssen, I need you to do me a favor and we'll jusss forget the shpeeding."

"Uh, sure."

"I'm thinking of running for sheriff myshelf one day and I'm having a little get-together at my house. I'd like for you to be there."

"Will there be cake?"

"You betcha. Now you're not obligated of courssse. I don't want you to think this is some kind of shakedown. I realize things come up, like Grand Jury duty for instance. Why, citizensss like you get called all the time."

"I'd love to be there." I said. "May I call you Sheriff?"

All of This for the Price of a Stamp?

Most people consider growing older a bad thing. Especially people approaching the big 5-0 and wondering if it's all that bad on the other side. Trust me; it sucks, but not all of it. Now, I'm not talking about gaining wisdom with age. I'm still pulling some of the same dumbass stunts I pulled thirty years ago. No, I'm talking about the wonderful stuff that keeps showing up in my mailbox. Luckily standard mail arrives at the pace it does or I'd be overwhelmed by the magnificent opportunities coming my way.

Today, for instance, I received a letter from a local hearing center informing me that I was one of thirty-five people selected for a manufacturer's field test of a brand new line of hearing aids. I didn't get opportunities like this when I was twenty-five.

The letter stated that these spectacular new hearing aids are specially designed to reduce listening efforts. Okay, this is where I had to say, "Huh?" Because I thought *all* hearing aids were designed for this purpose. But at my age, I'm certainly not going to question new technology.

All I had to do was make an appointment, and along with thirty-four other lucky people who cannot hear, I would receive this remarkable new device. But that's not all. I would also be getting something called a video otoscopy of my ear canal to see if my problem is merely wax build-up. I may have to invest in some Q-Tips. The audiologist will also give me a complete state-of-the-art hearing screening to determine if I'm beyond help. I may be so deaf that if didn't actually see the mushroom cloud I wouldn't know an atomic bomb just exploded.

Finally, if all goes well, I'll receive a thirty day free trial of these amazing contributions to the auditory sciences. I guess after thirty days you either pay up or the world shuts up. To think, I could walk past a couple of smartass teenagers and when they think I'm out of earshot one of them will say, "Hey, did you see the hearing aids on that old cocksucker?" I'll be able to hear that! Imagine how the quality of my life will be enhanced.

Another opportunity cast my way like a tied fly to a trout mouth is a chance to purchase my own rustic cabin nestled among the pines of the Blue Ridge Mountains. There, I can put my feet up beside a slippery silver river and try to coax my dinner from stream to pan. Ah, I can hear it now....

It all looks really good on the glossy paper it's printed on, but there are a couple of problems with this little scenario. Not the least being where in the hell do they get the idea I can afford my own rustic cabin nestled among the pines of the Blue Ridge Mountains? Especially after I put a down payment on my new bionic ears that apparently will let me hear the fish swimming underneath the water.

Another problem is I don't like to fish. I have friends who can sit on a boat or bank for hours waiting on a fish to give them the time of day. I do admire their high level of boredom. But when I want to eat a fish I go down to Captain Tom's and order the fried platter, with shrimp and flounder, coleslaw, baked potato, French fries, and Lord a mercy honey, can you bring me some more of those hush puppies?

By some miracle, let's say I did somehow catch a fish. I'd have to filet the son-of-a-bitch and fry it up. I'm no good at this shit. By the time the fish was ready to eat I'd be so hungry I'd swallow the damn thing whole, get a bone all hung up in my throat and there I'd be, flopping around on the patio with my mouth opening and closing, doing a great imitation of the fish I tortured not seven hours ago.

One more thing about that stupid cabin. After three days of blissful silence I'd be as crazy as a shithouse rat. Those voices in my head would finally have the control they've always wanted and, alternating between a whisper and a shout, would be saying things like, "Go ahead, go ahead you big nothing, buy that shotgun, look down its barrel into that deep dark hole.

What do you see down there? Paradise? Peace at last? Pull that trigger. If it was good enough for Hemingway, it's good enough for a hack like you." And they're right, oh dear God I know they are.

To get away from all that I drive into town and find the nearest bar. Being the new guy in town, a stranger, and unable to speak that fishing lingo I get into a tussle with one of the local good old boys. He pounds the living daylights out of me, causing me to lose one of my new hearing aids. I stagger home, half deaf and bleeding. The voices in my head are really whooping it up now because for them the party is just starting, and they've invited some voices over that I don't even know. Me? I sit on the porch of my rustic cabin and stare at that damn slippery silver river, unable to hear the fish anymore or even the birds singing as I contemplate that shotgun.

I threw the glossy ads in the trash.

The most interesting thing about getting older is you realize there are two great forces battling for your soul. Of course I'm talking about AARP and Generation America. Two organizations geared toward not only bettering the life of the retiree but also getting their fingers on the retiree dollar. AARP is the better known because they've been sending me letters and sample magazines for years in anticipation of my steady decline into feebleness. This tickled my wife to no end when she opened the mailbox and saw one of their invites for me to join. "You're going to be fifty soon!" Their chirpy little letters shouted out to the neighborhood. "Then your wrinkled old ass belongs to us!" I've hated AARP long before I knew they had a liberal agenda.

I've should have known about this before by all the famous people they splash across the covers of their magazines. But sometimes it's just so hard to think for myself. Instead of saying, "Hey, there's another entertainer with their screwy elitist politics on the cover of AARP." I was saying, "Damn, I didn't know Bruce Springsteen was that old!" But he is, and thanks to AARP, I now know growing old is cool.

Ever helpful to those of us who can't remember where we

parked our car, AARP has teamed up with the auto and health insurance industry to help save us money. Now please. I love and trust insurance companies as much as the next person. They've been steady as a rock for me over the years, consistently raising my rates when I've had the audacity to file a claim. AARP is trying to help the poor insurance companies out by herding its members toward someone they highly "recommend." It's not like there's anything in it for them. They have the senior citizens best interests at heart. Really. But there's no way the Association of Anal Retentive Pussies is going to get my hard-earned money, or my soul.

Generation America hasn't pestered me with anything in the mail yet so as far as I'm concerned this puts them up on any competition they may have. If they can afford to be aloof I'm sure their fee would be nominal to arrange for a young blond nurse named Inga to be sent over. She can feed me oatmeal and wipe my ass for me. They're probably thinking this service won't be needed by me before I'm ninety or so but I'm thinking why wait until I'm too old to enjoy it. Besides, later she can sit on my lap and read me my mail.

Bond, Uncommon Bond

Just the other day my wife, Denise, asked me to repair the porch railings. So naturally the first thing I did was sit down and turn on the television. Anytime you need to perform manual labor you're not getting paid for, such as fixing up your house or helping a friend move, your first order of business should be to sit a spell and gather yourself. This before you even touch a hammer and nails or attempt to lift an ottoman. You just can't rush into these things like a screaming banshee. Someone could get an eye put out. Work smarter, not harder. I can't tell you how much useless labor this little saying has saved me over the years. Why, sometimes it has gotten me out of doing anything at all.

So anyway, while I was putting on my porch-fixing shoes, I came across a James Bond movie. Bond, James Bond, was inexplicably convalescing in a wheelchair. It's disconcerting to see 007 in a wheelchair with a blanket over his knees. It's like seeing Superman driving a cab. It would be okay if the chair suddenly sprouted propellers or fired a surface-to-air missile. "Aha!" I would chortle. "I knew it was just a ruse." But he and the chair just sat there, an uncommon Bond for sure.

Soon, Bond was approached by a jabbering ninny whining about some international incident or another that could potentially blow the Earth to smithereens. I wasn't really following the plot closely at this point because most of my concern was focused on those pesky porch railings and the almost certain bloodletting I was about to endure. Bond appeared to be only slightly put off by this Earth-shattering information. The annoying ninny continued with his harangue for a minute or so, then two other guys showed up, plunged a hypodermic needle into his neck, and dragged his lifeless body away.

Enter a beautiful woman with serpentine eyes and thick, lustrous hair the color of mahogany. "James," She whispered in Bond's ear. "You can have me anywhere, anytime, and in any way you want." This led me to believe she was ready to give up the butt and I momentarily forgot about pounding nails. Unfortunately, this tender moment was interrupted by yet another man; this one with bad teeth and a briefcase. But he wasn't there to cause mischief, huh-uh. He acquired a password from Bond, James Bond and promptly transferred an impressive gob of money with many zeroes into 007's bank account.

All of this action took place in the span of about ten minutes, the same amount of time it took for my wife to tell me to get off my ass and come help her. "I'm on my way," I yelled back, lying of course, buying time as I tried to assimilate everything I had just witnessed. If any one of those things happened to me in ten minutes, make that ten months, even ten years. I'd be ecstatic and ready to accept whatever cruel twists fate had left for me.

Most guys at some point in their life dream of being James Bond, and the ones who don't, dream of being a Bond Girl. But that's another story for another time and a larger city. Being a realist, or as most successful people would call me, a "small thinker", I found it easier to try to equate Bond scenarios to my own life; not imagine actually being Bond. That whole "shaken, not stirred" thing, making love to all those exotic women, destroying flashy automobiles, and dispatching evil villains in new and progressive ways while wearing a tux is…well…doggone it…just too much work; plus people do tend to shoot at him.

I'm just not cut out for the spy business and would be way in over my head. Much like one of those big lottery winners that don't know what do with all that sudden fortune. They move to Florida, start cavorting with strippers and develop a fondness for cocaine. The money runs out and they're left drugged-out and destitute, with cravings they no longer can afford to satisfy. Give me my mundane life, interspersed with remarkable moments so subtle I'm not sure I didn't imagine them. Surround me with helpful, generous people so good at what they do that I don't even know they're there. My own guardian angels, protecting, gently nudging, and who don't mind shopping at Wal-Mart.

Let's say some irresponsible motorist short on time, patience, and common sense has been tailgating me mercilessly for the last five blocks. Finally, at the next stoplight, when it looks as if I've had just about enough, two men who look vaguely familiar, leap from a non-descript silver sedan, drag this unfortunate from his Cadillac Escalade and kick the living shit out of him for me. Pulling away I glance in my rearview mirror and note with satisfaction he is now bleeding from both ears. I give the guys a small nod thinking, "Well, Mr. Cad-E-Lack jackass, apparently I'm not the only one you've pissed off today." They continue their surveillance at a discreet distance. I sing along with the radio in ignorant bliss.

I love my wife. There is not enough allure on the planet, sexually or monetarily to make me risk what I have with her. Having gotten that disclaimer out of the way, it still doesn't mean I can't get a warm fuzzy feeling south of the belt buckle when a smoking-hot blonde gives me a little smile in an elevator. I'm thinking, "Yep...I still got it." She's thinking, "That old perv is giving me the creeps." Of course at that moment I don't want to think about what she's thinking. I just want to go on thinking that she's thinking, "For a guy of his age and heft, he's a highly attractive man." Just once, mind you, I'd like for this hot blond to lean over and whisper in my ear, "After we step off this elevator you can ravish me in the nearest available room." This would cause me to levitate briefly before I said to her, "I'm flattered, but sorry, I'm happily married." I would then exit the elevator, even if it wasn't my floor, find the nearest men's room, and slam my head on the edge of the sink repeatedly.

Like Bond, I too have had dealings with a man with bad British teeth and a briefcase. Unlike Bond, my experience resulted in me buying life insurance for my dog and loss protection against my cell phone. The dog eventually ate the cell phone and died but since the cell wasn't technically "lost" and the dog did not expire in the typical manner of most dogs, i.e. hit by a car, shot by irate neighbor, the "big sleep" needle, or dropping over dead while barking at a squirrel, neither policy paid off. This makes me reluctant to get into a long-term financial relationship with any character such as this. I definitely would not give him any of my passwords, even the one to Pandora radio. I can smell a scam as far away as Nigeria. But…if he was at the local pub and grub and wanted to saturate my innards with beer, then by golly, I'd let him.

"Who's your buck-toothed buddy?" Friends would ask.

"Who?" I'd say, feigning ignorance.

"That fella over there; paying for all your drinks."

"Oh him, he lost a bet."

He would continue to pull money from his briefcase and ply me with alcohol until I puked or fell down. It's just so hard to turn down free anything, especially if it's bad for you.

This is where the Bond movie faded to a commercial about a vacuum cleaner so light that the average woman could lift it with her tongue. It held my attention until I heard my wife do her heavy-footed mad walk down the hallway. I shut down fantasy land.

"What have you been doing, watching television?" She motioned to the remote still in my hand.

Dammit. WWJD. What would James do? Remain calm, of course. "I guess you expect me to talk?"

"No, I expect you to fix the porch railings before a group of Jehovah Witnesses falls into the bushes and sues us for everything we don't have."

Clever girl. I was trapped but maybe I could buy some time. I raised the remote control. "I was just going to check the weather. You wouldn't want to get started and have to stop because of rain, now would you?"

"Give it up." She slowly took the remote from my hand. "Now go."

I went. A good loser knows when he's beat. But there are other battles to be fought. There are gutters to clean and the house needs to be pressure-washed. But I am also ten minutes wiser and Denise doesn't know about my hypodermic-needle-bearing-angels.

Now That's Just Crazy Talk

Okay, you know and I know that the world is chock full of crazy people. We're surrounded by them. Think about it, but not for too long or you may become one of them. How many times a day do you find yourself having to deal with a person you're certain is a functioning lunatic? They're everywhere you know. They could be a co-worker, a neighbor, a family member, or someone in your writing class. Maybe you're sleeping with a person you suspect is unstable. You're not proud of it but the sex is good. It's okay, no one is pointing fingers here.

This morning you were on your way to work, minding your own business when suddenly the driver of the car in the lane beside yours decided she needed to be in YOUR LANE RIGHT NOW! Without as much as a glance she practically parked her silver Chevy Traverse in your lap. You missed her by inches. Your coffee went flying and you screamed out, in an octave you didn't know you could reach, "You stupid bitch! Watch where you're going!" Since anyone with a rudimentary understanding of English and four dollars can acquire a driver's license, someone almost runs your ass over on a daily basis. Still, it's not something you've grown comfortable with.

To settle your nerves you stop at McDonald's for a biscuit and hash browns. You only get to visit this cholesterol heaven once a week because your wife and doctor are on your ass about eating healthy. They have no idea that the thought of another salad for lunch sometimes makes you weep uncontrollably in the men's room. You've already pulled away from the drive-thru window when you realize the dumbasses left the cheese off your bacon and egg biscuit. You ordered cheese. You wanted cheese. What is bacon and egg without cheese? What kind of lousy service is this? And they're wanting $15 an hour? There's a good chance the unsmiling moron at the window gave you back incorrect change also.

You get to work, and before you can even get started checking to see which one of your favorite athletes got arrested last night, your boss jumps all over you for some other imbecile's screw-up. There's no need trying to reason with him or explain that you weren't even at work that day because your boss is the most complete, well-rounded idiot you know. He hates you because he fears you. You've heard that he thinks you're slightly unbalanced.

Now let's summarize, you've already encountered a stupid bitch, a bunch of dumbasses, a moron, an idiot, and an imbecile, and your day is just getting started.

Where do they all come from? Is everyone in the world out of their minds? Apparently they are, except for you and me of course. Secretly, deep down, we think we're the smartest people we know. Who's smarter? Nobody, that's who. There may be one or two people who you sometimes suspect may be just as smart but not really. Yeah, we're pretty damn sharp, you and me. Too smart to be self-delusional, that's for sure.

Time was, if you saw a man walking down the street with a wire sticking out of his ear, deep in animated conversation with what appears to be no one but himself, you would have thought he was insane. "That son-of-a-bitch is crazy. Let's cross to the other side of the street." Now it's commonplace. It's called technological advancement. But it also causes some confusion.

Suppose you're sitting at a stoplight and the guy in the car next to you is red in the face, waving his arms around, shouting at the empty interior of his automobile. You're thinking, "He must have Bluetooth and is talking to his priest." But hold on, he may be bonkers. Here's how you can tell. When he stops talking, watch him and see if he listens. If he listens intently, like he really cares about what he's hearing, he's talking to himself and is crazy as a damn loon. If he acts distracted and could care less about what is being said, yeah he's probably getting a sermon.

Craziness is relative to our own perception of accepted norms. I like saying stupid shit like that sometimes because it's fun. Crazy is crazy, you just have to be careful to use the correct word because there are so many levels.

I read on my computer at work where some baseball team was paying a player eighty-five million dollars to throw a baseball for five years. Not for five years without stopping mind you. He didn't even have to fling this baseball all day long or even every day. "That's insane," I thought. "I'd do it for half of that." But I was wrong. That wasn't insane, it was ludicrous. Insane would have been if he had turned them down.

The ex-sister-in-law of a fella I work with tried to rob a bank with a water pistol while at the drive-thru. Like artists, poets, fiction writers, and other manic depressives I found her work to be incredibly inspired. But what would be the word to describe such a person, really? Well, she's obviously not a half-wit because that would infer half of her has wit. My guess would be she's off her rocker, somewhat naïve, or a full-fledged damn fool. I bet she's interesting though and boy is she creative.

My co-worker didn't say what the result for this ill-conceived hold-up was but I'm betting the teller gave her the money anyway, per bank policy of not resisting. The would-be robber had already fired off a warning shot squirting water all over the glass window. "She means business. Everybody remain calm or someone will end up wet." Whoever made this bank policy could be classified as a dolt.

When asked why he robs banks, notorious criminal Willie Sutton replied, "Because that's where the money is." Willie clearly wasn't a dunce. Banks have money and sometimes they are held up by people with real guns loaded with real bullets. This could cause consternation with employees and customers. But from standing around talking to some of my co-workers while the boss was away, apparently six-year-olds playing cops and robbers using their little hands to simulate guns is also causing consternation? Why? I've never heard of anyone being killed by a finger. I've heard of people being killed because they *gave* someone the finger. Hey, the bastard went berserk, he deserved it. But enough violence, let's talk about love.

I was in a meeting at work the other morning trying to stay

awake when someone passed me a note. "A six-year-old boy kissed the hand of a female classmate and got suspended from school." it said. *Whoa.* I thought. *Sexual harassment. If the classmate he had kissed had been a male there probably would not have been a problem.* But that was just a foolish assumption...wasn't it?

I don't give much thought to time travel because that would make me a lunatic. But if someone from a hundred years ago suddenly appeared in my living room, wait, that wouldn't work, one of us would suffer a heart attack. No, let's just say I met someone on the street who was dressed funny and talking out of his head.

"Where am I?" He rants. "Am I in Hell?"

"No you're in Thomasville, a suburb of Hell. Where are you from?"

"I'm from Greensboro."

"That explains it."

"What year is this?" He looks warily around.

"2014."

"My God! My machine works! I've travelled 113 years into the future."

"Do you have any money?" I put an arm around his shoulders and steer him toward Christo's. Usually when I have conversations like this I'm drinking.

"I most certainly do. I'm not destitute."

Although his money was odd looking it was still American tender and that crazy Greek, Pavlo, was more than glad to take it. I've seen him accept a chicken for a shot of tequila. After about four or nine beers my new friend convinced me he was indeed from the year 1901. That's what I told him while he was still buying anyway. I'm not crazy.

He seemed to be fascinated by the "horseless carriages" zipping up and down the street. I told him about our flying machines and tried to explain the internet but he was going for any of that shit. He couldn't take his eyes off the TV above the bar. Those "amazing images" captivated him. I didn't get it. I mean "Dr. Phil" was on.

But what he really wanted to know about was society. He was obviously a people person.

"Please tell me about all the wonderful changes that have taken place, the progress of society." He says. "The world must live in peace and harmony now. Everyone educated, well-read and articulate. Communication must be highly evolved." He gestured with his hands. "I mean look at that marvelous invention." He pointed to the TV. There was a feminine hygiene commercial on. Jeez.

"Well, well, Percy, you've obviously taken leave of your senses my ignorant friend." I said. "Let me think for a second. As far as peace and harmony goes, people will pop a cap in your ass for a pair of tennis shoes nowadays."

"Pop a cap?"

"Yeah, you know, shoot, gun down."

"For a pair of shoes?"

"Well, they are $200 shoes."

"What!? Are people really that barbarous?"

"If you mean stupid, you damn right."

"That's mad!"

"I know, I know. You could find them a lot cheaper on Amazon."

"What about education? People have to be more learned."

"Do I appear *learned* to you?"

"Well, no actually. No offense."

"None taken. At least I can read. That's more than some high school graduates can say."

"What is that man doing over there with his head bowed over a device of some sort?"

"He's texting."

"He's Texan?"

"No, don't let the hat fool you. Texans don't wear cowboy hats with tennis shoes. He's a truck driver. No, he's *texting.* It's sorta like a telegram. He can send people messages and not have to actually talk to them. It's great. Let me tell you a little story about texting.

"The other day I was in Earl Ray's Guacamole Shack and

at the table beside me sat six people with their heads bowed. Out of respect I didn't order a Corona until they were through asking the blessing. But after ten minutes they still had their heads bowed and I'm thinking they must be Baptists. It turns out they were texting and tweeting. Six people at that table and not one of them could find a single person in the group they wanted to talk to."

"Why that's...that's... preposterous. You must be unbalanced or deluded in some way. None of this can possibly be. I must get away from you immediately. That's..."

"Crazy talk? I know it sounds like it but the world is chock full of crazy people Percy. They're everywhere. Look around you but don't make eye contact. Hey, maybe you're just having a bad dream."

As my new-found friend lurched out the door looking wildly about, I started laughing, softly at first before I launched into a full-fledged, slapping the bar, uproar. "1901, yeah right, that was a good one. I didn't believe that for a minute." I said aloud before I caught myself. I looked around. *These people must think I'm a psycho*, I thought. But no one was even paying attention to me, they were watching Dr. Phil.

If Wishes Were Fishes

I was standing outside the loading dock one clear-blue October afternoon calculating the odds of finding other employment before getting fired. This was more fun than actually working. One of the nameless girls who worked in the office came out to share a cigarette with me. Though technically I don't smoke, she was kind enough to blow her smoke in my face so I could enjoy it too.

Looking to break the keen silence that drew out between us like a married couple on a long car trip, she opened a line of conversation she figured all men were interested in, "You know my husband finished second in a fishing tournament this weekend." She cupped her elbow with her empty hand like her Marlboro Red was either too heavy to manage one-handed or she was afraid to let it stray too far from her face.

"Well he did pretty darn good," I said, mustering as much enthusiasm as I thought polite. It's not good to squander enthusiasm; you never know when you'll get it again.

"So where do you like to fish?" That she bothered to waste her, (more precious every day) breath on an obvious loser such as me told me she didn't like to smoke in silence. Apparently the sound of her lungs screaming in agony made her uncomfortable.

My first response to a question, any question, even if it's something innocuous like, "Are you wearing any underwear?" is to lie or exaggerate. "Why yes, I have one pair of underwear and I never take them off." Every time I make an exception, it invariably turns out wrong, biting me on the ass like some badly trained pet. For some unknown reason I replied with complete honesty this time. Perhaps I was trying to cleanse my soul. "Well, I don't really like to fish."

Her mouth fell open but this time but no smoke came out. "Are you a man?" she challenged, lowering her Marlboro. "I mean, really."

Luckily for me, not ten minutes earlier I had exited the men's room where I held in my hand an average-sized, mostly functioning, penis attached to my body near my very own scrotum. So I was able to answer quite confidently that I was indeed a man. "I sure am baby." I replied. "You want to cop a feel and see?"

Once more, luckily for me, she was fired for embezzling company funds before she could swing a sexual harassment charge my way. Dodging jail time by one of the over-processed hairs on her under-sized head left little time to concern herself about my manhood. "Are you a man?" Sheesh.

My wife tells everyone but me that I'm a real man, so there.

I was still left pondering though, do some people in this day and age equate catching, cleaning, and cooking your own fish with manliness? Yes, yes they do. Does it bother me, a little? Yes, yes it does. After doing a little soul-searching I realized maybe I was missing a tiny chip from my man gene. A real damn tiny piece mind you, but still...

The only thing I know about fishing is that I don't know anything about fishing. That's nobody's fault but mine. I've had numerous opportunities to learn but shunned them to do more fun things, like shoveling horse shit out of stalls. But I've decided to at least consider giving fishing a chance. You know the old saying "Give a man a fish and he will eat for a day but teach a man to fish and one day he'll have a boat he wants to sell."

From what I can piece together from intensive research, there are some contributing factors that would lead a person to choose fishing over other pursuits like golf or car restoration, or chess. First of all, golf is expensive, even on courses where a tee shot goes straight down the middle of the fairway and still lands in a big pile of cow dung. So there's that and also, golf balls are notoriously hard to eat.

We were dining out with some friends once enjoying the shrimp and whitefish combo down at Earl Ray's Fish Hut. Suddenly, without warning and un-provoked, Lester jumped straight up out of his chair, turning over a whole pitcher of good, sweet tea.

"What matter, Lestee?" asked his new Cambodian wife, Linny Lin, her eyes so big they were almost round.

"Gack!" Lester said, clutching his throat.

"You alright there, Les?" I was trying to get the waitress's attention because I was out of tartar sauce. My wife, meanwhile, was dabbing at the spilled tea with a big wad of napkins.

"Gack, gack!!" Lester was turning red and sweating profusely right there at the dinner table, for Pete's sake.

"He trouble! He trouble!" Linny Lin screamed, her tiny little hands waving around like butterflies.

That's when a stranger sitting at the next table, wearing a short sleeve, white, button-down shirt with a skinny black tie, leaped to his feet and said, "I think he's a'chokin." He grabbed old Lester from behind and yanked him so hard that both of Lester's feet came up off the floor. One of Lester's Sunday loafers went flying across the room and on the second yank he kicked the underside of the table so hard with his bare foot that, we found out later, he broke his big toe.

"Gackle!" Lester said after a large piece of fish and bone shot out of his mouth and landed very near his loafer. He bent over, wheezing and coughing, but getting his breath at last. The other diners applauded the badly dressed man and Linny Lin started crying. Oh boy, it was a sight to see. I never did get my damn tartar sauce and with service like that you can bet I won't be going back to Earl Ray's.

Anyway, after I thought about it, if that had been a Titleist jammed down in Lester's trachea we wouldn't have had to lug him to the doctor for a broken toe after we finished eating. No sir, I would have had to use one of my precious sick days to go to a funeral. I think that could be one of the reasons people prefer to fish.

The problem with working on old cars is, once again, the expense. If you're thinking, "Yeah, and spark plugs are hard to eat too," then you're just being silly. No one tries to eat car parts unless they're trying to get on TV.

My friend, Chavez, bought a '49 Ford coupe. Not a

particularly attractive car to begin with even in pristine condition. But he had a soft spot for that model because his mama got knocked-up in the back seat of one by a man she claimed was Chavez' father. That was as close as he ever got to his father so I wasn't about to tell him how damn ugly that car was.

He hauled it home from the junk yard and brought it back to its full, original luster, and painted it cherry red.

"So how much money you figure you've poured into this little hobby here?" I asked him one day as we sat in the back seat drinking beer.

"With the parts I had to track down, and labor," he said. "I've got about $81,743.32 tied up in it." He paused and looked off down the street for a moment like he had possibly forgotten to calculate a brake pad, or a strut or two. "No, that's about right." He nodded his head.

"How much do you expect to sell it for?" I had to ask because, though that might not sound like a lot of money to some people, it sounded like a lot to me.

"I'm hoping to get at least $15,000 out of it." He said. "I'd be willing to take a little less."

This may not make economic sense to someone outside the hobby. It almost appears that the government is heavily involved in some way. But, he seemed okay with it since some people believe you can't put a price on happiness.

Chess? Chess is played by stern looking men with pale hands and long, thin fingers. You know the type. Anyone else who plays wouldn't admit it. It'd be like walking into the local biker bar wearing a chartreuse sweater and announcing, "Hey guys, I knitted this myself."

Unlike chess, most everyone has a fond memory of fishing, except for people lost at sea, never to be seen again of course. Most other people think of Andy and Opie strolling down to the fishing hole with their poles resting on their shoulders, the quiet solitude spent beside a rushing stream, the big one that almost got away. Magical moments.

I have some of those memories myself before I grew old enough and big enough to say "Hell no, I ain't going fishing!"

Like the time I got stung multiple times by angry bees right
before I fell into that pristine river. You sure can't put a price
on happiness. Also there was the true pleasure of being woken
up at four o'clock in the morning by my older brother, raring to
go, while I was having one of those "special" dreams about
cheerleaders. I've tried to put any memory of fishing out of my
mind but then the other day I got to thinking about what that
thieving slut said to me at work and thought, "Well it might be
time to get another punch in my man card."

I drove down to Purvis's Purveyor of Piscatorial
Paraphernalia. A much wrinkled man, his skin earth brown, his
eyes the color of an undisturbed pond, stood behind a glass
display case. "Howdy." I said. This is the way fisherman greet
each other I've heard.

The gentleman said "Hello." He didn't smile.

He was wearing a battered hat that read "Abu Garcia" on
the front.

"Well, Mr. Garcia, may I call you Abu? I was hoping to get
started in the fishing business. Well not the 'fishing business'
per se, I mean as a hobby of course, or should I say pursuit?" I
was a little nervous and rambling.

"I'm Purvis," He said. "The name on the hat is a line of
fishing gear. You can call it whatever you like but most just
call it fishing." I could tell by his eyes he really wanted to add,
"You damn fool."

"I see. Well, Mr. Purvis where should I begin? I'm not real
familiar with all this, what did you call it, gear?"

"What kind of fishing are you planning on doing?"

A tough question right off the bat. I see severe people as a
challenge. I went for a joke. "I was hoping to do the kind that
involves water in some way."

Purvis frowned. "I mean fly fishing, bass fishing, lake,
river, deep sea, surf, from a pier, crappie, blue gill, trout, large
mouth."

"Gosh, I hadn't really thought about it. What would you
recommend?" Did he not say less than a minute ago that
fishing is fishing?

"Are you planning on doing it just for fun or are you looking to maybe fish some tournaments? Because if you want to fish in tournaments you're going to have to practice."

"Practice! Why in God's name would a person have to practice fishing? That's like practicing sitting on a porch swing."

"I'm starting to get the feeling you're making sport of my sport." He narrowed his eyes.

"Let's be honest with each other. Fishing isn't really a sport now is it. You don't have to be in shape or have hand eye coordination. Isn't fishing more like croquet, you know, a leisurely activity?"

"Mister, you've got a lot to learn."

I didn't know how to argue with a man wearing an Abu Garcia hat because I've never had to. "What I meant to say, of course, is I have no interest in fishing in a tournament. I just need a peaceful pastime that will help me sleep." I was feeling contrite now. "That looks like a nice rod over there."

"Now that there is a Diamond Back Jigging Rod."

I didn't know if I wanted to know what a jigging rod was but I had to ask.

"That's for fishing with a jig." Purvis thought he explained.

I've never been much of a dancer and I knew I sure couldn't pull it off while trying to catch a fish but I had to at least act interested. "How much is that bad boy?"

"$283.25."

"That sounds fair." I had no idea if that was a reasonable price or not but there was no way in hell I was plunking down three hundred dollars for a fishing pole. "That reel there in the glass case is a beauty. How much is it?"

"I got to give it to you mister," Purvis said. "You've got a good eye." He pulled the reel out laid it gently on the counter, his face aglow with pride. "This is a Shimano Stella 5000. I use one just like it."

"It's nice." I said, using my good eye. "How much is it?"

"Seven hundred and twenty-nine dollars and ninety-five cents."

"You've got to be shitting me!"

"Nope."

I would have stepped outside and took a swig out of my flask right then if I hadn't left it at home. I saw an electronic device over in the corner and asked old Purv what it was. I had just about decided to give up fishing before I even started but I wanted to leave here with at least a little knowledge gained in case I met that sweetheart I used to work with again I could talk the talk.

"That's a Fish Hawk 4D electronic fish finder. It gives you water temperature and such. You don't need something like that just starting out."

I didn't like his condescending attitude. "Fish finder huh? What does it do, find that special fish that's missing from your life, entice it to stick a hook in its lip?"

"Mister, don't mock a Hawk."

"I'm afraid to ask but how much is it?"

"It's $729.00 too."

I threw up my hands. "Okay, that's it. I'm outta here. I can't afford fishing either! I don't even know why I'm here to begin with. I don't like to fish, okay. There, I said it and I don't care who knows it, I'm still a man dammit! I heard Purvis pick up the phone as I huffed toward the door.

"Hold on mister." He said.

"What?" I stopped and turned.

"That was the Man Club. I'm going to have to take your card."

Two Rungs From the Bottom

I spent seventeen mostly unproductive years at my last place of employment. Like a tick on a dog's ass, in it for the long ride, I was bloated and happy. Then one day someone of much importance and little sympathy discovered me on the payroll. "Hey, what do we have here?" he said, and suddenly, I was plucked.

"Sorry to hear about the job there, Dan," a friend said. "What happened?"

"Well...I was downsized."

"Shit-canned huh?"

"Yeah, pretty much."

I quickly discovered there are worse phrases than being "stuck in a dead-end job" or "overqualified". "Out on the street" and "begging for change" and "dumpster diving" come to mind.

In desperate need of a paycheck, I answered an ad placed by a local restaurant that needed someone in the "promotions" department. I'd never been in restaurant promotion, or any other kind of promotion, as far as that goes, but how hard could it be? I'm outgoing, a self-starter, with a lot of big damn ideas. (My wife tells me that all the time. "Well you certainly have a lot of big damn ideas, now don't you?" It's good to have someone who believes in you.)

Perhaps this was a new beginning, the start of something good, and best of all, exciting. How great would that be? Maybe I could have my own office and wear a suit. I've never had a job where I wore a suit before. Except for those three days I worked at the funeral home and that doesn't count. Boy, talk about a dead-end job.

I called the Downtown Restaurant to set-up an interview. When I asked the girl who answered where they were located she responded, "Uh...downtown." When I became head of the promotional department, she would be re-trained, I decided.

Mr. Spiro, the owner, wheezing and puffing from the exertion of having to stand up, pointed to a chair when I walked into his office. I removed a stack of what looked like old menus, looking for an empty spot on the floor to put them.

"Just throw them anywhere," he said. "I've got more interviews today and we don't have much time."

That sounded ominous. I was going to have to bring my A game today.

He folded his large hands across a stomach that looked as if it had wrestled many a buffet into submission. His white shirt was open at the collar, the buttons testing the outer limits of the thread that held them. He looked me up and down for a moment, like he was sizing me up. I could hear seconds ticking away, never to return, slipping off to wherever it is that time goes. "What are you, about six feet?" He finally said.

"Yes sir."

"About 210 or so?"

"One ninety five," I lied. "Is that important?" I was thinking if it was I could amend my weight to closer to the truth. Get started off on the right foot and all.

"Not really." he said. "We can work with that. Jesus Christ it's hot in here today. Don't you think it's hot in here?"

"Yes sir, it is." I sat up straight, attentive, feet flat on the floor, and ready to give him all the answers he'd ever want to hear.

"Well, as you can see," he said, waving an arm around at the four walls of his cluttered office. "I'm surrounded by fast-food joints down here. There's one on every corner it seems like. Their food is crap but they've got advertising dollars out the wazoo and a name going for them." He leaned ponderously to one side and ripped off a long and loud fart. It was impressive by anyone's standards. "Excuse me." He said. "Anyway, people are basically like lazy cattle. It's easier for them to stumble in and order a number four with cheese than come in here for a nice sit-down. We serve good, quality food. You ever eat here?"

"I've meant to." I stammered.

115

"Yeah, well we've got competition out there and we need to make ourselves stand out. It's not good enough to have a superior product anymore."

Here's where I started getting excited, thinking of ways to get The Downtown Restaurant's name out there: newspapers, TV, radio. I felt like I was made for this job. "What exactly would I be doing Mr. Spiro?"

"Well, I'll be honest with you. I don't think you're cut out for this type of work. No offense, but this isn't everybody's forte."

"None taken, but if you'll give me..."

"What I'm looking for is somebody to stand outside our restaurant, on the sidewalk out there, dress up in a chicken suit and wave a sign around. I need them to really put their heart into it, entice people to come in here and try our hamburgers. The best damn burgers in town if you ask me. That sound like something you'd be interested in?"

Well, I wasn't getting an office but it looked as if I'd be wearing a suit after all. That's what the height and weight questions were about. The fat bastard was sizing me up for a chicken suit. "Gosh...uh...how...how much does it pay?" My voice sounded a little strangled to me.

"Come again?"

"The pay, how much does it pay?" Only a desperate man in desperate times would ask that question.

Mr. Spiro leaned back in his chair and locked his fingers behind his head. "Well..." he said, "that depends on your experience. Have you ever done this kind of work before?"

It felt really good, for the first time in my life, to be perfectly honest during a job interview. "I can sit here right now and truthfully say no I never have. To take the truth to the next level, Mr. Spiro, I've never even been asked to do this kind of work before, and frankly I never really expected to be. But I am a quick learner."

"Yeah, that's good." Spiro started rocking slowly back and forth, fiddling with a pen lying on his desk.

I felt I was losing his attention. I needed the job, that was certain, and part of me wanted the job too. I wanted to be the Downtown Chicken. It might look good on my resume' someday; performer. This is America. Who knows how far a man dressed up like a chicken can go? Look at that guy out in San Diego. He's made quite a career for himself. "So why a chicken and not a cow if you want to sell burgers?" I asked. This seemed like not only a reasonable question, but also showing an avid interest in the company and the direction it was taking.

He gave me the same look he must give his Mexican dishwasher as Juarez stands there in suds up to his elbows, shaking his head and repeating "No entiendo, no entiendo." A patient look, thinly stretched over grave irritation. "We sell more than hamburgers you know. Plus, haven't you ever heard of irony? You've seen the billboards where those cows are selling chicken? They can't spell for shit, but it's pretty damn effective. So why not a chicken selling beef? Plus a cow has that sack of tits all hanging out there. Who wants to look at that? You get it?"

I got it all right. "Does the chicken headpiece cover your face?" I was starting to feel confident, cocky even. I think Spiro lied about the other interviewees. After all, he had a bird in hand.

"No, no it doesn't cover your face. That would look weird. We need people to see your face so you can smile, make eye contact, set people at ease. We're a family restaurant. Why I bet kids will want their picture made with you."

So I'm out there, every day, with my whiteboard sign advertising daily specials. (They really do have good food. My wife has had to let my suit out once already. "You need to slow down on the country fried steak, bird boy." She says). I've got my own little dance and come on routine. I've also got a steady paycheck coming in every week. Yes sir, I'll give you a wave and dance you a jig. I'll flap my wings and give you a smile. The only thing I don't give is what some joker leaving the bar next door asks me at least once a week, "No sir buddy, I sure don't," I answer. "I don't give a cluck."

More Fun Than Death

This is the greatest idea in the history of mankind! Okay, that might be a small exaggeration but it's a better idea than a tattoo on your neck. Robinson's funeral home down in Easley, South Carolina is putting in a coffee shop serving Starbucks and food.

Now I never cared for paying five dollars for a damn cup of coffee, but you got to give them credit for trying to make someone feel better who just found out after kissing that old man's ass for five long years they still got left out of the will. They calling the new place "The Coffee Corner." Doesn't that sound cozy, Coffee Corner? It will have big fluffy chairs and a fireplace to sit by and ruminate about your freshly-deceased loved one and possibly contemplate where your own sorry ass is going to end up too.

Now all that's real slick and all, but here's the really good part: they will also have free Wi-Fi and big-screen television! My goodness, the only thing that could possibly make it better is beer, cold, and on draft, served in pitchers by pretty girls wearing them tight little shorts. Why they could even have happy hour. Of course, they couldn't call it that. But "Alive after Five Down at Robinson's" sure would be sweet.

When I read that Chris Robinson was the owner and proprietor, I got really excited because I thought this was the singer from The Black Crowes. I love me some Black Crowes. How much more better could this possibly get? For a small nominal fee, he could sing, "She Talks to Angels" for the mourners who are not only distraught, but also incredibly optimistic. If that didn't fit the mood he could whip up a rocking version of "Remedy" for the people who come down just to say good *damn* riddance. Unfortunately, I found out that this is not the same Chris Robinson, so we're stuck with a handshake and a "sorry for your loss." We still got the TV though!

Now Robinson's is more than just a fun place to meet friends for a Java Chip Frappuccino. They also provide a much-needed service, not only for the ones who have passed on and their entourage, but people who are still upright as well. Let's say there's absolutely nothing wrong with your phone service, but AT&T sends out a couple of jackasses named Buck and Silver Tooth to lay down new lines anyway.

While they out fiddle farting in your yard they cut the cable to your TV and internet services. Oh my God, you have no entertainment! Now what? What do you do now while the cable company takes seven to ten working days to give you your life, such as it is, back? Do you talk to your wife? Hell no! Play with your kids and help them with their homework? Absolutely not. You remember Robinson's has free Wi-Fi and you trot your ass on down there where the real fun is. Well, for some people. Everybody doesn't enjoy the same things.

Now Robinson's may have limited access to or even block those special websites you enjoy in the privacy of your own home. So you may have to wait until you actually laid out down there before you're stiff. Uh oh, I done went and said something nasty.

I foresee only one little tiny little problem with this whole sweet set-up, and that's football. Let's say it's football season, or worse, THE PLAYOFFS, and Robinson's is handling the arrangements for your loved one. You and your friends are glued to the 52" big-screen TV, having a swell time. There's fifteen seconds to go in the game, it's Baltimore 14 and Pittsburgh 10 but the Steelers have the ball on the Raven's three-yard line. Just at that moment your sister-in-law pokes her ugly nose through the door and says loud enough for everyone to hear, "The service is starting!"

Then you remember your wife, your wife, she wouldn't let you watch a game in peace when she was alive, and it don't look like she's going to when she's dead either. So you plead with your sister-in-law, "Please can it wait another fifteen seconds, please. I got fifty dollars on Pittsburgh and they getting ready to score!"

This could possibly cause conflict or, as some people are overly-sensitive, hurt some feelings. You may need to take Mr. Robinson to the side and ask him if the game starts running into overtime could he put your soul mate on ice until Monday. I'm sure this is another service they'll be glad to provide. As much as we don't like to think about these things, it's best to plan ahead and be prepared.

That this funeral home is in South Carolina is going to elicit all manner of comments from those people unfortunately trapped north of the Mason-Dixon Line. "Look at those damn hillbillies doing something else tacky and unrefined." You know they saying shit like this because they ain't had no home training. But we all know what that is now don't we? They be jealous, jealous again. Hey, ain't that a Black Crowes song too?

Hair Trigger

Someday, in the not-too-distant future, the last sliver of hair on my head will disappear down the shower drain. It will be missed. Until that day, I will consider myself to have hair, singular it may be, but hair nonetheless. The trick will be to get everyone else to buy into my self-deception.

I show up at work with my one hair spiked straight up to a dangerous point or lying at a jaunty angle. "Gee Dan; did you do something different with your ... hair?" lovely Brandy asks.

"Well," I reply sheepishly. "I did put a little mousse on it this morning. Going for that casual look, you know."

Or maybe I'm running late one morning and as I tear for the door my wife says, "You're not going out without combing your ... hair are you?"

"No," I answer, acting perturbed, but secretly pleased that she noticed. I then swagger off to the bathroom in search of my one-toothed comb.

A couple of friends, waiting for me at the stadium, spot me walking across a parking lot, the sun reflecting off my cranium like a car windshield. "Is that bald guy Danny?" one asks.

"Oh yeah, that's Danny alright, but he has hair." my other friend answers, my real friend, the one who cares, the one with two hairs left on his noggin.

Some men, brave and forthright men, see the inevitable and shave their heads, and because it's a law, grow goatees. This gives them that big biker/bar bouncer/badass look that would only get me pummeled in public. I don't want someone else choosing me as their evening's entertainment, even if it is for only a few violent seconds. As a matter of fact, I've been asked several times by considerate, thoughtful people, "Do you want me to kick your ass?" My answer has always been an enthusiastic "no!"

But that's not the reason I can't bring myself to take a razor to my skull. I wear glasses. Eyeglasses perched on my face under my large shiny head would make me look like an under-accessorized Mr. Potato Head. I suppose I could go the contact lens route but I can't stand the thought of sticking something in my eye, and then immediately having to stick something in my other eye. So with a slight case of misguided vanity, enough phobias for three people, and all those voices vying for attention inside my head, worrying about a "little" hair loss on the outside seems kind of vacuous.

"Hair loss" is actually a misnomer. I'm not *losing* hair. I have more hair now than any other time in my entire life. It has just migrated to other parts of my body, like my back for instance. I have a nice head of hair on my back. Strangely enough, no women have expressed an interest in running their fingers through it. Why? Hair is hair, what difference does it make where it's located? But it has made me more reluctant to take off my shirt, even in the shower.

Then there's the hair that has sprouted up on my ears like tiny porcupine quills waving in the wind. I purchased a snazzy hat to cover my low tide hairline, a la Tim McGraw and I suppose I could find one to cover my ears, a la Elmer Fudd, but instead I opted for a set of electric clippers. That's what I need, more time in the bathroom, alone, doing something else weird. Like giving my ears a buzz cut. If someone had told me at twenty-five I would be doing this someday, I would have laughed the good laugh. I would have laughed and swept my hair back out of my eyes.

But I don't have to live with hair loss. That's what the commercial said, "YOU DON'T HAVE TO LIVE WITH HAIR LOSS." The announcer sounded very sincere. There were photos of a bald guy looking downward, unsmiling, and wearing an ugly shirt. Then there were pictures of the same guy, un-bald and smiling, looking the world in the eye after his amazing HAIR RESTORATION. His taste in clothing had improved quite a bit also. He swam and his new transplanted hair remained in place, wet, shiny, and oh-so-thick. Then he jogged and played basketball. Apparently you have a lot more energy when you have hair.

Of course they had the good looking babe, young enough to be his daughter, running her fingers through his brand new mane of hair, practically cooing, "I'm ready for sex now." But my favorite part was the scene of him blow-drying his new hair. He had that baby on full hurricane force and I'm shaking my head thinking, "He's gonna blow that mess right off his head and into the toilet" but no, his impressive new follicles hung on for dear life. "What would a full head of hair do for my appearance and self-confidence?" I wondered aloud. Could I finally jump into the deep end of the pool?

I asked my friend Jenny, whose opinion of men I truly respect because she so much wants to be one, "Jenny what do think of bald guys?"

"You're asking *me* what women think of bald guys."

"Well, yes."

"You're a strange man, Danny, but I think most women want their men to have hair."

"What about me? Would I look better with more hair? You have nice hair by the way."

"You'd be less ugly if that's what you mean, and thanks."

Feeling giddy with, and intrigued by, the possibilities, I researched hair restoration, quickly scanning the internet looking for words like "painless", "natural-looking", and most important "inexpensive". Instead there were words like "local anesthesia" and "injection", words I've always associated with "pain". There was a bunch of troubling information about hair transplant procedure, actually. After "injecting" the "local anesthesia" the surgeon removes a three to four inch strip of scalp from the victim's head, sets it aside and then sews the scalp shut. So, the first step is to painfully *remove* hair. This was puzzling so I kept reading. The surgeon then divides the strip of scalp into 500 to 2000 tiny grafts each containing one or a few hairs. This must be time consuming, driving up costs, unless the surgeon has a handy Scalp Dicer Deluxe that is only available to real medical professionals.

Using a needle or scalpel, the surgeon then pokes tiny holes in the head and delicately places a graft in each hole, like rows of little saplings above a well-furrowed brow. I'm not a doctor but in my humble layman's opinion this has to hurt like mortal hell. This torture could take up to eight hours and for more fun, if your hair continues to fall out or you want more hair, *you may have to do it all over again*. It depends on how much pain you and your wallet can endure, as this surgery costs $4,000 to $15,000 and is not covered by insurance.

After reading this far, I was totally convinced that "bald is beautiful" and I could live with grabbing a hat for a trip to the mailbox, but the clincher was after two or three weeks, *the transplanted hair falls out*! According to the article though, you *should* be seeing new growth in a few months. Here you've laid down $15,000 for new hair that you're supposed to be able to swim with and it *falls out with no guarantee it will grow back*? I've been snookered into carnival games with better odds than that.

The article stated that you could return to work after about five days of lying around your house wrestling with misery and doubt. This is where the real fun begins. Your co-workers don't ask about your "hair" but instead stare at your red and puffy scalp, "What in the devil happened to your head? Did someone bury you up to your neck in sand and then forget about you?"

Your whole life becomes a big deception. You want people to think that you have nice hair but have it to look so "natural" that nobody says, "Hey, have you always had hair?" But after three weeks it all falls out anyway so nothing has really changed but your bank account and the way people look at you.

"First he didn't have hair, then he had hair, and now he doesn't have hair again. What the hell is going on with him?" They whisper behind your back. "Is he, like, smoking crack?"

They may whisper, but you hear anyway and you think, "I'll show them. In six months I'll have hair Fabio will envy." Then that little voice that you hate says, "Yeah, if it works."

Months pass and then one day you wake up and your scalp is inflamed and infected where the new hair is sprouting up!

"What is this, Doctor?" You practically scream over the phone.

"Not to worry, I already cashed the check." He says. "Ha ha, just kidding. It's called folliculitis and it's just a temporary condition."

You call your boss and say, "I can't come in today I have folliculitis."

"Wow," He says. "Do you know who gave it to you?"

"I sure do. It cost me $15,000."

"Wow," He says again. "She must have been a looker. Were you in Vegas? Wait, I'm not supposed to ask that."

"Oh yeah, she was a hottie all right." See, you'd rather your idiotic boss think you have an STD than admit you got a hair transplant.

Let me review: I spend a truckload of money on an operation that may or may not work, is very painful for a long period of time, and could be potentially embarrassing by drawing unwanted attention to my ever-changing hairline. Hmmm…that is a quandary but I think I'm going to have to pass.

So it's back to square one. As much as I want to believe it, one hair doesn't mean I *have* hair. What do I do, age gracefully into that gentle wisdom expected from old farts? No more sarcasm? No more wise ass remarks? God help me, I'll go friggin' insane. "Who's that crazy old bald bastard that lives at the end of the street?" People will ask.

"Oh he hasn't always been crazy." Someone will answer. "He used to have hair."

Fore!

So there we all were wasting another Saturday at the Bent Elbow Golf & Country Club. An outsider might take a look at "The Elbow" and laugh that it has the gall to call itself a "country club". This is a joke they would laugh at only once, and not for any noticeable progression of time, because to us it is a club. If you turn your nose up at it you turning your nose up at us and we don't like that much. Not at all really.

They ain't no swimming pool here and the clubhouse is barely more than a barn with a couple or three dozen golf balls for sale and some old beat up clubs you can rent...or borrow. It might take more than one of them old golf carts to get you around our nine holes twice. The course itself looks like a patched green quilt coming apart at the seams. But if a man can put his hand around enough cold malt liquors and close his eyes for a moment, the wind shifting those pines sound just like it does down at Augusta, I bet. And golf...well, you know, golf is golf, no matter how much you pay.

When I say "we", I means me (Big Cletus), Teddy (some still call him Little Teddy), and Earl. We were waiting on our fourth, Willie. We always waiting on Willie. I started to ask Willie once why he didn't buy a watch but stopped myself because I knowed the fool probably couldn't tell the time anyway. If he didn't have somebody always telling him, "Willie you better hurry up or you gonna be late again." He'd never get anywhere at all, just stay in one place, inert, like a small stone, stepped on or kicked to the side. Willie's a damn fool.

The three of us were standing on the practice putting green, missing putts and talking about nothing, watching the parking lot because we had a tee time in about ten minutes. Just because our little nine-hole layout won't be in no travel magazines don't mean we don't like to keep things regular. I was getting ready to line up another putt when Teddy called me to the side. "Big Cletus," He said. "Come over here a minute."

"What is it Teddy?" I was irritated a bit because grown men shouldn't be whispering like children.

"Well," He said. "The other day I rented an adult movie and I saw my ex-wife in it."

I was a little taken aback by all this information, beings I didn't really want to hear it in the first place. "What did you say Teddy?"

"I said. I saw my ex-wife in an adult movie!"

"Are you sho' it was her?"

"Yeah, I'm sho'. She has a birthmark on her ass that looks just like a exclamation mark. I've seen that mark from every angle known to man. When the cameraman zoomed in for a close-up I said, "Yep, that's her alright, that's her."

"So how do you feel about this Teddy?"

"Well...I feel a lot of ways. But surprised ain't one of them."

"I can't say that I'm surprised myself but you must be a little hurt maybe, or disillusioned, disappointed?"

"Yep, He said. "That, and that, and that too. All that."

In trying to ascertain the depths of Teddy's emotions I discovered he still had feelings for this woman and stopped to ponder my next words. You see I'm sort of a diplomat around these parts. Ask anybody, they'll tell you, "Big Cletus is a fair and rightful man. He coulda been a diplomat to a difficult country."

In the meanwhile, Earl, who had overheard us because his nose is as long as it is wide, ambled over. "So, Ted, yo' wife is in a X-rated movie huh?"

"It's my ex-wife but yeah the movie is X-rated." Teddy stuck his chin out a little bit.

"Hmmm...Well what's the name of this here movie?" Earl asked.

"What damn difference does that make?"

"Oh nothing," Earl said and turned to walk away. "Just never mind."

"Hey, wait a damn minute! You want to see my wife naked, don't you?"

"Ex-wife," Said Earl.

"Ex-wife then, you've always wanted to see my ex-wife naked."

"No, it's not so much that," Earl said. "It's just that I don't want to be the only one that hasn't."

I stepped between them.

Just at that moment we heard a car backfire, a horn blow, and looked around to see Willie running across the parking lot with his clubs in one hand and his golf shoes in the other. "Please," I thought. "Please don't let him call out my name in front of all these people standing around out here. I don't want them to know I know him."

"I'm coming Big Cletus," He yelled. "I'm coming."

Damn.

After much discussion and no small animation it was decided, rightly so, that Willie would ride in the same cart with Earl and I would ride with Teddy. We get to the first tee and agreed to play a dollar a side, first on the green, first birdie, first par, pays a dollar; second hole out draws first up on next tee, sand saves are fifty cents, three putts pay out and four putts are a wash. That's on the odd holes; even holes everything is reversed. It's a simple game to keep up with and wager on so that's why we play the same way every time.

Earl sliced his drive over in the woods, the same damn place, like he always does; Willie hits a little ol' pop fly about 125 yards but it is straight and he's all bragging about how it's "right down the middle." Teddy is a little upset still and tops his drive barely over what would be the women's tee if there was any womens who played here. That made Willie laugh very loud. I really, really don't like Willie. I busted my drive right down the middle about 250 yards because I can play this damn game.

After three holes, if my math was correct, I figured I was up about seven dollars or so. This was the way it was supposed to be. Teddy was a little morose and I started to tell him to forget about it and move on. He had a new woman in his life now. His ex-wife had certainly moved on and from the sound of it had several new men in her life. I was getting ready to tell him this very thing when I saw Earl talking real low to Willie, pointing, and grinning at Teddy. I was hoping we could go ahead and tee off but we had to wait on the fourth tee for a group ahead that was playing worse than we were.

Willie saw this as an opportunity to saunter up to Teddy and say, "Sooo…Little Teddy, I understand your ex old lady is doing porno now."

Teddy gave Earl a look but said to Willie, "She's an actress."

I felt my knees loosen a little bit on that one despite myself.

"Actress?" said Willie. "No no Little Teddy. She's a ho. And she was a ho befo. So…why you so low when you shoulda know?"

Willie thinks himself some kinda rap star when he's really just a full-fledged fool. But my knees did loosen some more. I had forgotten my job was to further diplomatic relations.

Teddy has a brand new Big Bertha driver with a graphite shaft and a titanium head that has a sweet spot as big as his girlfriend's ass. Of course he can't hit it worth a damn. I'd like to get my hands on it and hit it a couple of times. The driver I mean, not the girlfriend's ass. Ted's got enough problems right now. He took the Big Bertha, reached up and whacked Willie in the head with it. For good measure he gave Willie a couple of shots to the nads too while he was at it. Diplomatically speaking, I thought that wwaas a little low. In retrospect a three iron would have done more damage but driver is what Teddy had in his hand at that moment. It sounded like it hurt plenty enough though; especially applied numerous times like it was.

"Help me Earl!" Willie cried out; one arm over his head, one hand covering his crotch, neither giving much protection. Earl didn't want none of what Willie was getting, he remained in the cart. Teddy kept on whaling, whaling on Willie, and his boys. "Big Cletus, make him stop!" Willie looked to me but my knees done buckled I was laughing so hard. This was better than an eagle putt.

Well Willie done seen enough of Teddy's new titanium driver with the graphite shaft and took off down the fairway the best he could with Teddy in hot pursuit. They reached the dogleg and kept on going straight into the woods. "Man, Teddy done drove one into the woods. Teddy's getting good distance with that Big Bertha." I joked to Earl. He didn't smile. He was still in the cart.

I teed up my ball and hit 250 yards right down the middle because, you know, I can play this damn game. "That'll play." I said. "That'll play nicely."

Me and Earl finished our round and I won a few dollars. That's the way it should be. I reckon next week about this time we'll be wasting another Saturday down at the Bent Elbow Golf and Country Club. We might have to find another fourth though. I suspect Willie might not be able to join us. Men in full body casts tend to be inert, like a stone. And that's the way it's supposed to be, at least at the Bent Elbow Golf & Country Club.

Weekend Trip

Although conservative in nature, Mabry likes to visit a city in the western part of the state that is quite liberal in its views. The town's vibe suits him, even though its live and let live attitude is always at war in his soul with "Why can't these damn heathens straighten up and act right." He also loves the beautiful art, music, and women which the town holds an abundance of. Every other street corner is a small stage for someone strumming the blues or fiddling a jig. "Disney World for grown-ups," is the secret thought that brings a smile. A friend asked once why he would want to go there since it was full of nothing but "old hippies and queers". His friend's summation bothered Mabry none because the town always made him feel young. No easy feat at his age.

This particular weekend the streets were closed to traffic for something called the Bele Chere Festival, which took the normal carousing to an even higher plane. After a day and evening of partying, eating, and drinking, he and his wife, Ursula, took a cab back to the hotel to rest up for the following day, round two. Somewhere between the lobster crepes, corndogs, and microbrews he developed a case of heartburn from the pits of Hell.

"Here," Ursula said to him as he collapsed into bed. "Take this Zantac."

"I don't want a damn Zantac," He said because he's a rebel at heart, even though at the moment that rebel heart was on fire. His wife, rightly surmising you can't argue with a drunk, placed the pill in his hand and dropped the subject. He drifted off into a dreamless sleep.

At 4 a.m. he awoke with what felt like a lump of burning coal in his chest and remembered the Zantac. At this point he would have gladly popped a cat turd in his mouth if it offered some relief. The Zantac was no longer in his fist so I felt around under the covers until his hand closed around a pill

131

which he swallowed eagerly. Unfortunately this was not a pill manufactured for the relief of heartburn.

Earlier in the day his bed was changed and made up by a Gabriella Santos whose boyfriend, Carlos, had a penchant for hallucinogenic drugs. He liked to take Gabriella on these little trips with him whenever she would come along. They revisited the Montes de Maria without having to hail a cab. In the course of putting clean sheets on the bed, a hit of potent purple mescaline fell from her pocket unnoticed. He discovered it twenty hours later, groping in the dark, looking for some relief.

Relief was not what he found.

In about the same amount of time it takes to get a pizza delivered to your door Mabry was experiencing thoughts, sounds, and sights uncommon to his cul-de-sac existence. Carlos would have explained to him in perfect English that "You're tripping your ass off man."

Eyes open wide, he scanned the room in glorious paranoia. *I'm never eating food from a street vendor again*, he thought. *I'm getting sick. What's that!? Is that a pair of feet sticking out from under that curtain? Is someone standing behind the curtain? No, wait, they're behind the other curtain! Should I get up and hit them with a chair? No...I don't want to wake Ursula. No, that's a crazy thought. Of course she'd want to know if there was an intruder in our room. What's wrong with me? Okay, those aren't feet they're just shadows. There is nobody behind the curtains. Whew! I bet they're behind the bathroom door! I'll get up and see. No, that's too far to walk right now although...I bet I could teleport.*" That image caused him to bark out a small laugh and he immediately clapped a hand over his mouth. Ursula stirred but did not awaken.

Okay, he said to himself, his eyes were drawn back to the shadows that looked like feet or the feet that looked like shadows, he couldn't remember which. *Is it curtain number one, curtain number two, or door number three? Hey, what was that old show with Monty Hall, Truth or Consequences? No...no...LET'S MAKE A DEAL!!* He shouted out loud, which, as any married man can attest, is the last thing a slumbering wife wants to hear at four-thirty in the morning.

"What's wrong, Mabry?" she slurred. "Are you having a nightmare?"

"I have stumbled upon a revelation not even worthy of trivia." Mabry said, in his best imitation of Alex Trebeck.

"Mabry, wake up, you're talking out of your head."

"Sleep will not be my companion this morn. I am off to explore the world's barely hidden secrets. Meanwhile, the All Man Psycho Band is warming up in the wings." With that he leaped from the bed and headed for the door dressed only in his Fruit-Of-The-Looms and Defiant Jester t-shirt.

"Mabry, are you sleepwalking?"

He turned to the black lump on the bed that represented his wife and said, "My dear, I've never been more aware of anything in my entire life. I'm going out." He opened the door and stepped out into the near dawn.

"Close the door behind you." Ursula said, too tired to argue.

Mabry ambled down the sidewalk toward the pool marveling at all the different notes the birds sang. "Why have I never noticed that before?" he wondered. He looked into the trees and saw octaves, half-notes, sharps, and flats, falling from the branches like ill-shaped leaves. He no longer felt sick, as a matter of fact he'd never felt better in his entire life except for what sounded like the low humming of a tightly strung wire in the back of his head.

"Well," he thought he heard a voice say softly. It sounded like Morgan Freeman. "You must be as strong as a bull to have eaten and drank the way you have all day and still feel this vibrant. Maybe the years are regressing from you and tomorrow you'll be younger than today."

"Maybe I..." He laughed aloud and turned to the person speaking to him. There was no one there. The rest of the sentence died on his lips. He looked quickly around. He was alone but felt like he was being watched, which he was.

There was a security camera aimed at him sending an image back to a monitor casually scanned by a bored and sleepy desk clerk named Kimberlee Nicholson. She was curious as to what the near-naked man was doing wandering around in the parking lot but not enough to call security and definitely not enough to go see for herself. She decided to keep an eye on him as long as he was on camera. Besides, he looked harmless.

The heebie jeebies were getting the best of him and he was ready to return to his room when he heard singing. It was the Beatles, "All You Need is Love", except they sounded a little off key, very much like he did when he sang in the shower. *Hmmm...* He thought. *I'll have to tell Ursula later how much the Beatles sound like me and also remind her that all you really do need is love. She doesn't need a new dishwasher. I know she'll appreciate my insight."*

Still singing softly to himself, even though now the sound appeared to be coming from over the mountain and far away, he made his way to the pool. *You know, swimming underwater is as free as flying except you don't have to worry about crashing to Earth.* He thought. *Of course the ocean has a bottom and the sky has no ceiling that we know of unless you're already in the sky looking down and then the Earth would be...the ceiling, or the floor? Damn, simple thoughts are more complicated than tricky ones. No matter, I think I'll fly, but to be free I must be totally free.* He slipped off his tighty whities and stood naked at the pool's edge. Inside the hotel office Kimberlee picked up the phone.

He looked at the inviting water and then scolded himself. *You know you need to walk around naked more often. You look magnificent.* Yep Carlos, he really was tripping. "Now ladies and gents it's time to fly." He leaped awkwardly into the deep end of the pool, smiling the whole time, even as the cold water enveloped him. He was free, free to swim to the depths. He was agile and buoyant; if only he had gills he'd never have to surface. It was only when he touched bottom that he remembered he couldn't swim. Screaming to the surface, he let out a yelp before swallowing a mouthful of chlorine-laced water. "Hep me!" he shouted. "I can't swim!" At five o'clock in the morning no one heard. God not only loves drunks and little children but apparently also first-time trippers because he managed to lurch and flounder his way to the shallow end of the pool and drag himself out. There, he lay staring at a discarded cigarette butt ringed in red lipstick and proceeded to have a rip-roaring laughing fit.

After ten minutes of free-falling mirth he snapped his laughter off and sat straight up looking warily around. *Something's afoot.* He said to himself. *They're coming.* He had the feral instincts of a wild animal. It was time to high tail it back to his room. He picked up the cigarette butt "for evidence", and still naked, made his way to room 119, knocking on the door with a soft rap.

Inside room 119 two people lay in an uneasy false sleep. Like the old country music song, they were married, but not to each other. Oneka Hoskins thought she heard a light knocking on the door but hoped it was her imagination. She knew her husband was getting suspicious and she was trying to find a way to break it off with Terrance. At first it had been new and exciting, now it had grown old and she was weary, tired of the lies and deceit it took to try to please two men.

Terrance Place lay beside Oneka, his restless itch scratched, and wrestled with his own mean-spirited thoughts. *How am I going to ditch this clingy bitch without a scene?* It was time to move on.

There came a harder rapping on the door and Oneka sat straight up. "Someone's out there!" she whispered hoarsely.

"Well, no shit," said Terrance.

"Who do you think it is?"

"I left my x-ray vision glasses at the house. How the hell am I supposed to know?"

Outside room 119 Mabry was getting pretty pissed thinking of Ursula lying in bed snug and warm, ignoring him on purpose while he stood outside naked and cold. *Where are my clothes, by the way?* He wondered again. I started banging on the door hard and loud. "Open the door you damn bitch!" He yelled. He didn't normally speak to his loving wife in that manner but he wasn't himself that morning, he was several selves, none of them him.

"Oh my God, it's my husband!" Oneka cried inside room 119. It didn't sound like her husband but between her guilt and fear, his apparent anger and the muffling of the door, she couldn't tell exactly. Besides, who else could it be? Oneka didn't formulate all these thoughts in her head at once because, well, she's not bright and it was early. By the time all this registered in her brain, Terrance was standing at the window with the curtains pulled to the side looking out.

"Is your husband an old white dude with a pot belly?" He looked at Oneka with a small amount of disgust.

"No! What do you think I am?"

"Open up! I know you're in there," Came through the door followed by more banging. Mabry's short-lived anger had dissipated and all of a sudden he was having fun again. *I'm an actor in a play.* He thought. *I've returned from the war and I'm here to re-claim my saucy wench.* He couldn't wait to share this with Ursula, maybe she would play along. He reached to knock on the door again when it opened. Stage-acting and saucy wenches but not war were temporarily forgotten as he was suddenly confronted by a large and angry black man.

"What do you want, fool?" The man said.

"Hah," Mabry said, getting back into character. "What are you doing in there with my wife?"

"Your wife is not in here!"

"Is that so?"

Terrance, feeling tired and a little mean stepped aside enough for Mabry to see inside. "Does that look like your wife?" He pointed to Oneka who sat on the bed, her lovely brown breasts exposed.

"Oh me, oh my, look at those chocolate boobies," Mabry exclaimed.

Before she covered herself up Oneka thought that breaking up with Terrance wasn't going to be so hard after all, as a matter of fact it was going to be a pleasure.

"Hey! Mabry said. "What did y'all do with my wife?"

"Get the hell out of here!" Terrance said, and with that picked Mabry up over his head and tossed him in the bushes.

As the branches painfully scraped and prodded his naked body and dusty leaves closed around him, Mabry felt as if the bush was eating him alive. Bugs scurried over his legs and chest and the more he thrashed, trying to get out, the further he sank down into a green oblivion. "Hep me!" He yelled for the second time in less than thirty minutes. "I'm being eaten alive!" Although his chance of dying this time was next to none, providence still intervened and a hand reached down from above. Inside room 119 a loud but painless breakup of an illicit romance began.

The hairy helping hand that hefted Mabry from the holly bush was attached to the arm of Glen Atkins which was attached to the body that Glen fervently wished was anywhere but right there, right then. Normally at six o'clock in the morning Glen was polishing off his last cup of coffee, writing "no incidents to report" on his third-shift detail sheet, debating whether to hit the free breakfast buffet, or head straight home to Molly, his cocker spaniel. Any options he usually enjoyed without any outside debate were taken away this fine morning, all choices removed.

Glen hated working in security only slightly less than he hated starving, which is what he would be doing if not for this God forsaken job. Knowing this job had him by the balls made him hate it even more. It had a few perks, Kimberlee was sweet and so were the free eggs and hotcakes, but mostly it just reaffirmed how dependent he had become. Glen was the most insecure security guy this world held. Confrontation was just a hard word to spell for Glen; not something he practiced nor needed to. Most people slept on third shift, including Glen.

When Kimberlee called saying there was a naked drunk in the pool he figured the guy would be "froze out" and back in his room by the time he got there so Glen saw no need for haste. When he discovered the drunk still naked, scratched and screaming in the bushes, Glen was perplexed. Seeing no other way out of this scenario he did what he hoped someone would do for him someday if he fell in the bushes, he extended a hand.

Mabry took the hand and hauled himself out of the man-eating bush with shaky relief. "Great gonzo, my Samaritan rescuer, danger lurks in every corner of this sideshow."

"Sir, are you okay?" Glen stepped back and assumed what he hoped was a position of authority, feet shoulder width apart, hands folded in front of him in a non-threatening manner.

"Besides a near-drowning, attacked by a brute with anger issues, and almost being devoured by shrubbery I'm mighty fine; except for THIS!" Mabry thrust the lipstick-rimmed cigarette butt at Glen who flinched and threw up his hands.

"What is it?" Glen almost shrieked.

"Well it's obvious what it is. It's a clue left by someone who commits crimes that require cunning and bravado but who got a little careless this time around."

Glen took the "clue" from Mabry and looked at it with trepidation. He may have to file a report on this too. "I don't understand." he finally said.

"Oh, but you will," Mabry said. "Find the owner of this little souvenir and you'll discover someone with more than just a nasty habit and bad manners; you'll find a criminal that's been pursued for ages. You do watch TV don't you?" At this point Mabry had moved from the physical to the metaphysical. He thought he had achieved genius, spouting wisdom that he hoped would fall on the correct ears. This was wasted on Glen.

"Sir, are you a guest of this hotel?"

"I most certainly was until my room was taken over by people whose first reaction to adversity is violence."

"Which room is that sir?"

"Why that one right there, the one with all the noise emitting from it." Mabry's ears were finely-tuned. Besides the Beatles he could also hear the Bells of St. Peter's Basilica, 4,695 miles away. Give or take a foot or two.

Glen turned to where Mabry was pointing and finally heard the rigmarole coming from room 119. He didn't really want to knock on that door. Maybe that argument would peter itself out. These things generally do. Meanwhile he had an unstable person on his hands that in ten minutes he could pass on to Bobby, the first-shift security guy. Glen would just lead him to the office put a robe on him, sit him a down and say "sayonara crazy person, my world awaits." With any luck Bobby would have to fill out the report and deal with the police. "Sir, you'll need to come with me." He reached to take Mabry's arm.

For the first time Mabry saw Glen's uniform and badge and shifted from intellectual to wild animal bent on survival. Not being a violent man there was no chance of fight, only flight, Mabry decided to skedaddle. "No lackey servant of a Socialist state shall take me to a dark cell where I'll never be seen again!" This is what he thought he said, what actually came out was, "Shit!" He took off running, with the grace and speed of an antelope, once more only in his mind. In reality Glen could have caught him easily if he had wanted to, but why bother when he saw all his current trouble loping away from him? Most problems don't solve themselves so easily. Glen was as happy as a minimum wage earner could be.

The door to room 117 opened up and Ursula stuck her head out just in time to see a hairy, bare ass turn the corner of Olive and Magnolia. "Mabry!" she yelled without enthusiasm. She saw a new side of the man she had wed twenty-one years ago and she well...she kinda liked it. Besides he'd tucker himself out in another block or two, limp back, and they'd have coffee.

"Ma'am," Glen said. "Do you know that gentleman?"

"Not at the moment." Ursula answered. "Not at the moment." And she certainly spoke the truth.

Finally, the last rightly thinking molecule clicked into place in Mabry's tormented brain. Or as Carlos would say, "You crashing man." The twenty miles he thought he had fled was actually only a couple of blocks; does a wife understand her husband or what? He scurried back to the hotel with early-morning drivers blowing their horns and yelling encouragement. It's a pretty free-thinking town.

"Do you still have heartburn?" Ursula asked, handing him a cup of coffee.

"I don't know." He said as he sat down on the side of the bed looking around. "Where are my clothes? What happened to me?"

"I think you had a bad dream and went for an extended sleep-walk. Here take this, you'll feel better."

"It won't make me crazy will it?"

"Nah, it's just a Zantac. Are you tripping or something?"

Birthday Surprise

When we look back at our friend Andre's most recent birthday party, most of us remember it with a tear in our eye. It was that special. As surprise parties go, this one certainly fit the bill. Andre was indeed caught off guard, but as it turned out he wasn't the only one.

The planning went off without a hitch. There were no furtive glances or poorly concealed whispers. The conversation didn't suddenly change timbre or subject when Andre entered the room. No one asked out-of-character questions or pretended they didn't know his birthday was coming up soon. Everyone acted just so doggone normal. Andre suspected not a thing.

It's hard to get a large group to agree, to organize, to follow one lead. That responsibility fell to Gillian, Andre's wife, who normally didn't possess the skills to organize an orgy, but this year, by God, she was focused. This party needed to be pulled off without a hitch. This party was just...needed.

It had been a mostly tumultuous year for Andre with a few peaks and a lot of valleys. He lost his job of seventeen years but soon found another, so for a compact space of time he was looking skyward again. But he began coming down from that particular mountain when he realized this was just another job going exactly nowhere. He had not a single friend at work, all his co-workers were standoffish, aloof, or downright cruel. When someone asked about his job his first order of business was to stifle hateful words and homicidal thoughts. He'd smile then and say, "It's fine. I'm thankful to have a job."

Then death came and took a friend, then another, and another, until Andre didn't see life anymore, all he saw was another day in front of him, another step in the march toward the grave. All the good people were taken away while the low-lifes and the dregs remained unaccountable. It was an unfairness he could barely abide. Many times he wished he could just wave his hand and they'd all just die. He was in large need of an attitude adjustment. Luckily he still had plenty of friends to spare, and Gillian. Gillian loved Andre very much and kept the demons on the other side of the door when she was around.

Probably the best friend Andre had was Charlie. Andre thought Charlie, if not a genius, easily the smartest person he knew. "There's nothing Charlie doesn't know or can't do." He liked to tell his wife. What made it even more impressive, in Andre's mind, was Charlie's humility.

"I don't really know what I'm talking about," Charlie would say. "I'm just good at faking it."

One of Charlie's interests, probably his biggest actually, was weaponry. It was his area of expertise. Crossbows, knives, blowguns, rifles, shotguns, and pistols filled his conversation. Andre was never that big on owning a gun of any type; didn't have an aversion to them, just not much of an interest. But Andre wasn't stupid, not on purpose anyway. He heard the news and, unless you live somewhere the world can't find you, so have you. There are crazies out there with a lust for innocent blood. The more innocent the better it seems at times.

Andre wasn't a scared man, sometimes he was a nervous man, but he wasn't a coward. He wasn't concerned about protecting his life, he was worried that he couldn't protect Gillian, their home, and the life they had. "We need to get a gun." He told her one day. "We live in a safe neighborhood but you never know. It's something I hope I never have to use, but I'd rather have it and not need it as need it and not have it. You just never know." His argument sounded weak in his own ears but his conviction burned deep. And Gillian agreed because she loved Andre and despite the demons scratching on the other side of the door, this side was sweet and funny, and good.

Charlie put a pistol in Andre's hand and took him shooting. Andre discovered that a gun was innocuous in itself, no more dangerous than a smart phone, and a lot of fun to blast holes in targets. He was hooked. "People really do kill people," He thought. I thought that just NRA propaganda. Anything can be a weapon when handled the wrong way." It's an amazing thing to watch, a man's confidence blossom at that age.

"You have a birthday coming up," Gillian told Andre, noting the look in his eyes when he talked about shooting targets. He seemed to be heading for a peak again and it's so much easier to fly from there. "Why don't you find a gun you like and that'll be your birthday present?" She had many other things planned for his birthday but he didn't need to know everything, did he?

Andre found a pistol he liked, an Argentine-made Bersa Thunder ACP .380 single-action/double action in duo-tone. Most of that seemed like gibberish but he did like the way it looked and felt in his hand. He became surprisingly proficient with his new toy, so comfortable with it he obtained a concealed carry permit and practiced his quick-draw when alone, (the gun always safely empty, always) morphing from Barney Fife into Matt Dillon. "This is how the west was won," He whispered to the full-length mirror in his bedroom, miraculously never murdering his image.

The day of the party, a Saturday of gentle sunshine, arrived and since Andre and Gillian celebrated Andre's birthday the previous Thursday with a quiet dinner at his favorite restaurant, a party never once entered his mind. He was in the comfortable, familiar zone of same, nothing to get worked-up about. Still he was nervous and on edge and he didn't know why. That's what demons do. They find your quietest moments to whisper, cackle, and cajole.

"Are you going shooting with Charlie today?" Gillian asked.

"If you don't mind."

"Of course not. It's still your birthday weekend you know." That Gillian, so sweet and cagey.

Though every other nerve in his body prowled like a leopard on a leash, his eyes and hands were like granite. The bulls-eye never had a chance. Andre and Charlie rode home in the twilight, an easy banter lilting between the good friends.

As they approached the front door in the closing darkness Andre said, "Gillian must be at her mother's. It's funny she didn't leave a light on though. I guess she thought I'd be home before dark." Dear Andre was incorrect on that assumption. His wife knew almost exactly when he would walk through that door. What she didn't know was that the demons were coming with him; they had finally kicked down the door.

Stepping into darkness, lights suddenly flashed in Andre's eyes. "Surprise!" Blinded and scared, there were unexpected people in his house and he was outnumbered. But he had seven full metal jackets in the magazine and one in the chamber, if he was going down it would not be alone. Like lightning out came the Thunder. Aiming for the torso, the largest target, he saw no faces and heard no screams.

The first shot ruined Gillian's party dress with a big red unexpected corsage in the center of her chest. She crumpled without a sound. Round two hit his boss Dave in the left shoulder spinning him around and landing on the birthday cake. He survived to testify. Andre's third shot hit his neighbor Ted in the stomach. Ted bled to death looking at a water stain in the ceiling that he and Andre had discussed repairing just last week. Andre was high with his fourth shot because he was jostled by his sister-in-law fleeing for the door. The bullet found a mark though, ripping the left ear off of a pretty fourteen-year-old named Allison Cornell, who begged her mom not to make her go to the party because it would be just a "lot of boring old people."

Charlie, finally gathering his wits, tackled Andre on his sixth shot, the bullet finding the kneecap of Max Paulson, Gilllian's ninety-year-old grandfather who already needed a walker to get around. Needless to say, Mr. Paulson never got out of bed again for the six weeks he remained alive. Shots seven and eight remained where all their brothers should have stayed, un-fired and in the gun. Yes sir, it was a party to remember.

****

I don't really know anyone named Andre, or Gillian, or

Charlie for that matter. I had a childhood friend named Charlie, but we don't talk anymore. I woke up from this dream the other night, sweating and scared. Since it's pretty lonely at two o'clock in the morning, I woke up my wife as well. "Honey," I said. "Do we know anyone named Andre?" I heard a heavy sigh.

"No Danny, go to sleep."

"Okay, but do we own a gun?"

"Yes, Danny, it's in the nightstand. Please don't make me use it. Go to sleep."

"Good." I rolled over and went back to a dreamless sleep, smiling as I dozed off, feeling safe, feeling sound.